STUDY GUIDE
TO ACCOMPANY

PROFESSIONAL

BAKING

Sixth Edition

Wayne Gisslen

WILEY

John Wiley & Sons, Inc.

Library of Congress Cataloging-in-Publication Data:
ISBN: 978-1-118-15833-3

Printed in the United States of America
10 9 8 7 6 5 4

Contents

To the Student

This manual is a companion to the *Sixth Edition* of *Professional Baking*. Its purpose is to help you study and review the material in the text.

Learning to bake and to prepare pastries and desserts is to a great extent a practical, hands-on endeavor. Much of your training involves learning manual skills by practicing them under the guidance of an instructor or supervisor, and then improving those skills by repeated practice.

These practical skills, however, depend on a large body of knowledge and understanding. You need to know about such essential matters as gluten development, characteristics of various flours and other baking ingredients, measurement, formula structure, and procedures for preparing the basic doughs, batters, creams, and fillings. Using this manual will help you study and master this material.

This study guide is arranged by chapter, corresponding to the 27 chapters in *Professional Baking*. Each chapter contains several exercises that you can use to test your knowledge. This manual will help you see what you have learned and what you need to review. The following are guidelines for using the different kinds of exercises.

CHAPTER OBJECTIVES

Each chapter's learning objectives are repeated, as they appear at the beginning of each text chapter. They are not exercises, but they are included here as a reminder of the specific skills you should be learning in each chapter.

TERMS

The first exercise in each chapter is a list of definitions or descriptions of terms used in the bakeshop. In each of the blanks provided, write the term that is defined or described.

This is the only kind of exercise you will find in every chapter. Why is there so much emphasis on terms? It is important not only that you learn how to bake, but that you can communicate with other bakers and cooks. A food service career involves teamwork and sharing of information. To communicate, you must know the language of the bakeshop and kitchen.

COMPLETION, SHORT-ANSWER QUESTIONS, AND OTHER WRITTEN EXERCISES

Many exercises ask you to fill in blanks with words or phrases or to write out various kinds of answers.

If the problem is a regular question, a space is provided in which you can write out the answer.

If the problem is a statement that contains one or more blanks, fill in the blanks so that the statement is accurate and makes a complete sentence.

If the problem asks you to write a procedure or to explain how to do a task, write out the procedure using numbered steps. You do not need to *explain* each step, the way the text sometimes does, but be sure that your procedure is complete. Don't leave out any steps.

TRUE/FALSE QUESTIONS

For each question, draw a circle around the *T* if the statement is *completely* true. Draw a circle around the *F* if the statement is only *partly* true or is *completely* false.

MATH EXERCISES

Math is very important in the bakeshop and the pastry kitchen. Throughout your career you will have to make many kinds of mathematical calculations. Some of the most basic of these are explained in *Professional Baking*.

Some of the most important calculations you will have to make in the bakeshop involve converting formulas to get different yields. This is done using a system of percentages, as explained in Chapter 2. Calculations involving baker's percentages are included throughout this workbook, to give you practice.

Another kind of math problem you will find throughout the book involves calculating unit costs for bakeshop formulas. Again, the procedures for solving these problems are explained in Chapter 2 of the text.

Other kinds of math problems are included in appropriate chapters. Whenever you have difficulty with any of the math problems, turn to the explanation in the text and review it.

These are the kinds of exercises you will find most often in this manual. There are also other kinds of problems and questions that are especially included to help you review the material in a particular chapter. The instructions at the beginning of each of these sections explain how to do the problems.

Chapter 1
The Baking Profession

This chapter gives an overview of the baking profession. In the first part of the chapter, you will read about the development of baking from earliest times to the present. In the second section, you will learn about the many possible career paths open to trained bakers and pastry chefs, including some you may not have considered previously. Finally, you will find a discussion of the personal characteristics that are important precursors to achieving success in the baking profession.

After studying Chapter 1, you should be able to:

1. Describe the major events in the history of baking, from prehistoric times to the present.

2. Name the principal career positions in modern food service and bakery operations.

3. Name and discuss four attitude characteristics possessed by successful bakers and pastry cooks.

A.   TERMS

Fill in each blank with the term that is defined or described.

_____   1.   French term for a person who makes ice cream.

_____   2.   An elastic substance made up of proteins in wheat flour.

_____   3.   French term for pastry chef.

_____   4.   French term for a person who prepares show pieces, sugar work, and decorated cakes.

_____   5.   A cooking style that uses ingredients and techniques from more than one regional cuisine in a single dish.

_____   6.   French term for a bread baker.

_____   7.   The name of the Frenchman who started the first restaurant in Paris.

_____   8.   The name of the modern method of flour milling in which the grains are broken between metal rollers.

_____   9.   French word for a cook.

_____ 10. The great French chef of the beginning of the twentieth century who simplified and systematized classical cooking and reorganized the kitchen.

_____ 11. The greatest chef of the early nineteenth century, known for his contributions to the art of the pastry chef, as well as to refining classical cooking.

_____ 12. French term for pantry chef.

_____ 13. The worker in charge of production in a retail bakery.

_____ 14. French term for confectioner or candy maker.

_____ 15. French term for the person in charge of kitchen production.

B.   SHORT-ANSWER QUESTIONS

Fill in the blanks as required.

1. The earliest grain foods made by prehistoric people probably consisted of _____

   _____

   _____

   _____

   _____.

2. Describe how the first yeast-leavened bread probably came into being.

   _____

   _____

   _____

   _____

3. In ancient and modern times, flour made from what grain was the most expensive, and thus, eaten primarily by wealthier people? _____

4. In ancient Greece, foods were divided into two categories: bread and _____

   _____.

5. In ancient Rome, the primary fat used in making pastries was _____ and the primary sweetener was _____.

6. True or false: Most bread in the Middle Ages was homemade. _____ Why or why not?

   _____

   _____.

2

7. During the Middle Ages, the only people allowed to bake bread for sale were

    _____.

8. Refined sugar originally came from what part of the world? _____

9. From the point of view of pastry makers, the most important new food product that became
    available after the European discovery of the Americas was _____.

10. In addition to the product described in question 9, what other essential baking ingredient
    became more widely available after the European discovery of the Americas? _____

11. The first two major books on bread baking were published in the country of _____
    in the last half of the _____ century.

12. In the Middle Ages, why was white bread more expensive than whole-grain bread?

    _____

    _____

    _____

13. What does the repetitive nature of much bakery work give the baker the opportunity to do?

    _____

    _____

    _____

Chapter 2

Basic Professional Skills: Bakeshop Math and Food Safety

Measurement is one of the most important skills in the bakeshop. The success of the formulas depends on your ability to measure ingredients accurately. Closely related to this skill is the ability to perform mathematical calculations with those measurements. This chapter provides an explanation of these important techniques.

The second part of this chapter introduces another set of vital bakeshop skills: food safety and sanitation. Here you will read about the concepts that will help you protect the health of your customers, your coworkers, and yourself.

After studying Chapter 2, you should be able to:

1. Describe the problems and limitations of written formulas.

2. Describe the two basic functions of standardized formulas.

3. Explain the importance of weighing baking ingredients.

4. Use a baker's balance scale.

5. Calculate raw fruit yields based on trimming losses.

6. Use formulas based on baker's percentages.

7. Convert formulas to different yields.

8. Calculate edible portion (EP) unit costs.

9. Calculate formula costs.

10. Describe steps to prevent foodborne diseases in the areas of personal hygiene and food-handling techniques.

A. TERMS

Fill in each blank with the term that is defined or described.

_____ 1. A baker's term for weighing, usually of ingredients or doughs or batters.

_____ 2. Containing a harmful substance that was not present in the food originally.

_____ 3. A substance in food that can cause illness or injury.

_____ 4. Prefix in the metric system meaning *one-hundredth*.

_____ 5. Prefix in the metric system meaning *one-thousandth*.

_____ 6. Prefix in the metric system meaning *one-tenth*.

_____ 7. The basic unit of length in the metric system; slightly longer than 3 feet.

_____ 8. Prefix in the metric system meaning "one-thousandth."

_____ 9. Basic unit of volume in the metric system; slightly larger than 1 quart.

_____ 10. Basic unit of weight in the metric system; equal to about one-thirtieth of an ounce.

_____ 11. The initials of a formal food safety system of self-inspection designed to highlight hazardous foods and control food handling.

_____ 12. The transfer of bacteria or other hazard from one food to another or from equipment or work surfaces to food.

_____ 13. The weight of an item as purchased, and before trimming.

_____ 14. The weight of an item after trimming.

_____ 15. Requiring an absence of oxygen to live and grow; said of bacteria.

_____ 16. Able to live and grow either with or without oxygen.

_____ 17. A set of instructions describing the way a given establishment prepares a particular dish.

_____ 18. The basic unit of temperature in the metric system.

_____ 19. The basic unit of temperature in the U.S. system of measurement.

_____ 20. A microorganism that causes disease.

_____ 21. The temperature range of 41° to 135°F (5° to 57°C), in which bacteria grow rapidly.

6

B. UNITS OF MEASURE

For each of the following abbreviations, write out the full name of the unit of measure in the space provided.

1. lb   _____

2. mL   _____

3. qt   _____

4. dL   _____

5. oz   _____

6. pt   _____

7. tsp   _____

8. g   _____

9. gal   _____

10. cm   _____

11. kg   _____

12. tbsp   _____

13 L   _____

14. mm   _____

15. cL   _____

Fill in the blanks by making the correct conversion.

16. 6 fl oz   =   _____ tbsp

17. 3¾ lb   =   _____ oz

18. 9 tsp   =   _____ tbsp

19. 20 oz   =   _____ lb

20. ½ gal   =   _____ pt

21. 1½ cups   =   _____ fl oz

22. 2½ fl oz   =   _____ tsp

23. 1¾ pt   =   _____ fl oz

24. 10 tbsp   =   _____ fl oz

25. 48 fl oz   =   _____ qt

26. 4½ lb   =   _____ oz

27. 60 oz   =   _____ lb

28. 0.1 kg   =   _____ g

29. 2300 ml   =   _____ L

30. 1.6 kg   =   _____ g

31. 6 dl   =   _____ ml

32. 12 cl   =   _____ ml

33. 1750 g   =   _____ kg

34. 150 ml   =   _____ L

35. 750 g   =   _____ kg

C. TRIMMING LOSS

The exercises below are of two kinds: calculating yield and calculating amount needed. To do the calculations, you need to know the percentage yield for each fruit, as listed in Chapter 22 of the text. For your convenience, the necessary percentages are repeated here.

Apples	75%
Apricots	94%
Cherries (pitted)	82%
Coconut	50%
Grapefruit (sections)	50%
Grapes	90%
Kiwi fruit	80%
Mangoes	75%
Watermelon	45%
Papaya	65%
Peaches	75%
Pineapple	50%
Plums	95%

Calculating Amount Needed

Assume you need the following quantities, EP, of the indicated fresh fruits. Calculate the AP weight you will need to get the required yield. Items 1–10 use U.S. amounts; items 11–20 use metric measures. Determine whichever amounts are assigned by your instructor.

	EP Weight Desired	AP Weight Needed
1. Grapefruit, sectioned	1 lb 4 oz	_____
2. Plums	1 lb	_____
3. Kiwi fruit	2 lb 8 oz	_____
4. Pineapple	15 oz	_____
5. Peaches	2 lb	_____
6. Apples	5 lb	_____
7. Cherries, pitted	1 lb 8 oz	_____
8. Mangoes	12 oz	_____
9. Grapes	1 lb 8 oz	_____
10. Papaya	2 lb	_____

	EP Weight Desired	AP Weight Needed
11. Grapefruit, sectioned	600 g	_____
12. Plums	450 g	_____
13. Kiwi fruit	1200 g	_____
14. Pineapple	425 g	_____
15. Peaches	1000 g	_____
16. Apples	2200 g	_____
17. Cherries, pitted	750 g	_____
18. Mangoes	360 g	_____
19. Grapes	750 g	_____
20. Papaya	900 g	_____

Calculating Yield

Assume you have the following quantities of the indicated fresh fruits. Calculate the EP weight you will have after trimming. Items 21–30 use U.S. amounts; items 31–40 use metric measures. Determine whichever amounts are assigned by your instructor.

	AP Weight	EP Weight
21. Coconut	5 lb	_____
22. Apricots	2 lb	_____
23. Watermelon	10 lb	_____
24. Apples	4 lb 8 oz	_____
25. Kiwi fruit	1 lb 4 oz	_____
26. Grapefruit, sectioned	2 lb 4 oz	_____
27. Mangoes	1 lb 12 oz	_____
28. Papaya	2 lb	_____
29. Grapes	3 lb 4 oz	_____
30. Peaches	6 lb	_____

	AP Weight	EP Weight
31. Coconut	2200 g	_____
32. Apricots	900 g	_____
33. Watermelon	4500 g	_____
34. Apples	2000 g	_____
35. Kiwi fruit	600 g	_____
36. Grapefruit, sectioned	1000 g	_____
37. Mangoes	800 g	_____
38. Papaya	900 g	_____
39. Grapes	1500 g	_____
40. Peaches	2700 g	_____

D. USING BAKER'S PERCENTAGES

Use the percentages given to calculate the quantities needed in the following formulas. You are provided with either the weight of the flour or the total yield by weight. Fill in the blanks with your answers. Do either the U.S. or metric calculations, or both, as directed by your instructor.

I.

	U.S. Measures	Baker's %	Metric Measures
Butter	_____	67%	_____
Sugar	_____	115%	_____
Salt	_____	1.5%	_____
Unsweetened chocolate	_____	33%	_____
Eggs	_____	50%	_____
Cake flour	12 oz	100%	375 g
Baking powder	_____	4%	_____
Milk	_____	50%	_____
Vanilla	_____	2%	_____

II.

	U.S. Measures	Baker's %	Metric Measures
Water	_____	50%	_____
Yeast	_____	3%	_____
Flour	_____	100%	_____
Malt syrup	_____	6%	_____
Salt	_____	1.5%	_____
Oil	_____	0.5%	_____
Yield	9 lb 10 oz	161%	4425 g

III.	U.S. Measures	Baker's %	Metric Measures
Water	_____	40%	_____
Yeast	_____	5%	_____
Shortening	_____	25%	_____
Sugar	_____	20%	_____
Salt	_____	1.25%	_____
Eggs	_____	15%	_____
Bread flour	3 lb 12 oz	75%	1800 g
Cake flour	1 lb 4 oz	25%	600 g

E. CALCULATING FORMULA COSTS

Cost out the following formula. For the prices of ingredients, use figures supplied by your instructor or taken from the Sample Prices in the Appendix of this Study Guide. The problem is given in both U.S. and metric measures. Complete the problem assigned by your instructor.

Item: Scones

Yield: 6 lb 8 oz

Ingredients	Amount	Amount in Converted Units	EP Unit Cost ($)	Total ($)
Bread flour	1 lb 8 oz	_____	_____	_____
Pastry flour	1 lb 8 oz	_____	_____	_____
Salt	0.5 oz	_____	_____	_____
Sugar	6 oz	_____	_____	_____
Baking powder	3 oz	_____	_____	_____
Butter	1 lb 3 oz	_____	_____	_____
Eggs	7 oz	_____	_____	_____
Whole milk	1 lb 5 oz	_____	_____	_____
		Total cost		_____
		Quantity produced		_____
		Cost per lb		_____

Item: Scones

Yield: 2634 g

Ingredients	Amount	Amount in Converted Units	EP Unit Cost ($)	Total ($)
Bread flour	600 g	_____	_____	_____
Pastry flour	600 g	_____	_____	_____
Salt	12 g	_____	_____	_____
Sugar	150 g	_____	_____	_____
Baking powder	72 g	_____	_____	_____
Butter	480 g	_____	_____	_____
Eggs	180 g	_____	_____	_____
Whole milk	540 g	_____	_____	_____
Total cost				_____
Quantity produced				_____
Cost per kg				_____

Chapter 3

Baking and Pastry Equipment

Bread baking and pastry making require a great deal of equipment. Some of this equipment is familiar to any cook. Pots, pans, and knives, for example, are used in the bakeshop as well as in the kitchen. At the same time, there also is a lot of specialized equipment that is used primarily in the bakeshop. This chapter provides an introduction to this special equipment, from mixers and deck ovens to baking molds in many shapes. You will not be using this equipment all at once, but you should have a general understanding of the kinds of tools available to you for the many tasks you will be required to perform now and in the future.

This chapter is devoted entirely to the identification and description of equipment items and their uses, so there is only one section of exercises: Terms.

After studying Chapter 3, you should be able to:

1. Identify good safety and sanitation practices for purchasing and handling bakeshop equipment.

2. Identify the principal pieces of large equipment used in baking and pastry making, and indicate their uses.

3. Identify the principal pans, containers, and molds used in baking and pastry making, and indicate their uses.

4. Identify the principal hand tools used in baking and pastry making, and indicate their uses.

5. Identify other important pieces of equipment used in baking and pastry making, and indicate their uses.

A. TERMS

Fill in each blank with the term that is defined or described.

_____ 1.   A mixer, with a removable bowl and beater attachment, that spins around its own axis while revolving in an orbit to reach all parts of the bowl.

_____ 2.   A machine that cuts a "press" of dough into smaller, equal-size pieces.

_____ 3.   A covered loaf pan for baking bread that yields square slices.

_____ 4.   A stainless steel ring used for making molded desserts and shaping and holding desserts made up of layers of cake, pastry, and fillings.

_____ 5.   A small, boat-shaped mold.

_____ 6.   A dome-shaped mold for frozen desserts.

_____ 7.   A mixer with a spiral beater attachment and a rotating bowl.

_____ 8.   A machine that cuts a "press" of dough into equal portions and then shapes each portion into a ball.

_____ 9.   A machine that forms dough into sheets by means of rollers and a conveyor belt.

_____ 10. An oven in which breads and other goods are baked directly on the floor of the oven.

_____ 11. A type of refrigerator that maintains a high humidity to prevent doughs from drying.

_____ 12. A bentwood basket used for proofing loaves of bread.

_____ 13. A stainless steel pan for holding foods in service counters; also used for baking and steaming items such as bread pudding.

_____ 14. A ring- or doughnut-shaped mold for baking a yeast item of the same name.

_____ 15. A cake pan with a removable bottom.

_____ 16. A deep pan with a tube in the center, used mainly for baking angel food cakes.

_____ 17. A baking pan with shell-shaped indentations, used for baking small cakes of the same name.

_____ 18. A tool, consisting of a handle attached to a rotating tube fitted with spikes, for piercing holes in rolled-out dough.

_____ 19. A thin, flat board with a long handle, used for inserting and removing hearth breads from ovens.

_____ 20. A tool for measuring the density of syrups.

_____ 21. A mixer attachment used for mixing and kneading yeast doughs.

_____ 22. A machine that rolls and forms pieces of bread dough for standard loaves, baguettes, and rolls.

_____ 23. A box used to produce the ideal temperature and humidity for fermenting yeast products.

_____ 24. A large oven into which entire racks of sheet pans can be wheeled.

_____ 25. A steam kettle that can be tilted.

_____ 26. A small plastic tool, usually triangular, with edges cut in different patterns, used for decorating or texturing icings.

_____ 27. A round, flat disk that swivels freely on a pedestal; used for holding cakes for decorating.

_____ 28. A sheet of heavy linen or canvas, used for holding certain types of breads, such as baguettes, as they are proofed.

_____ 29. A flexible, nonstick liner for sheet pans, made of silicone and reinforced with fiberglass.

_____ 30. A conical strainer with a fine mesh, used mostly for straining sauces.

Chapter 4
Ingredients

A baker must be thoroughly familiar with the basic ingredients of the bakeshop in order to handle them properly in production. This chapter introduces you to these ingredients and their most important characteristics. Special emphasis is placed on the properties of various flours, which are, of course, the baker's primary ingredients.

After studying Chapter 4, you should be able to:

1. Understand the characteristics and functions of wheat flours and identify their main types by sight and feel.

2. Understand the characteristics and functions of other flours, meals, and starches.

3. Understand the characteristics and functions of sugars.

4. Understand the characteristics and functions of fats.

5. Understand the characteristics and functions of milk and milk products.

6. Understand the characteristics and functions of eggs.

7. Understand the characteristics and functions of leavening agents.

8. Understand the characteristics and functions of gelling agents.

9. Understand the characteristics and functions of fruits and nuts.

10. Understand the characteristics and functions of chocolate and cocoa.

11, Understand the characteristics and functions of salt, spices, and flavorings.

12. Make appropriate adjustments in formulas when substituting ingredients, such as dry milk for liquid milk and dry yeast for cake yeast.

A.   TERMS

Fill in each blank with the term that is defined or described.

_____ 1. Any of a group of solid fats, usually white and tasteless, that have been specially formulated for baking.

_____ 2. The chemical name for regular granulated sugar and confectioners' sugar.

_____ 3. The process of beating fat and sugar together to incorporate air.

_____ 4. A mixture of solid fats and other substances intended to resemble butter.

19

_____ 5. Flour made from the entire wheat kernel minus the bran and germ.

_____ 6. A mixture of two simple sugars, dextrose and levulose, resulting from the breakdown of sucrose.

_____ 7. A heavy brown syrup made from sugarcane.

_____ 8. The process of whipping eggs, sometimes with sugar, to incorporate air.

_____ 9. A flavoring ingredient consisting of flavorful oils and other substances dissolved in alcohol.

_____ 10. Flour from soft wheat with a low protein content.

_____ 11. Flour from hard wheat with a high protein content.

_____ 12. A dark, coarse meal or flour made from entire rye grains.

_____ 13. A tan-colored wheat flour made from the outer portion of the endosperm.

_____ 14. The process by which yeast changes sugars into alcohol and carbon dioxide gas.

_____ 15. The hard outer covering of kernels of wheat and other grains.

_____ 16. The plant embryo portion of a grain kernel.

_____ 17. A type of syrup, extracted from malted barley, containing maltose sugar.

_____ 18. The production or incorporation of gases in a baked product to increase volume and produce shape and texture.

_____ 19. The product that results when cocoa beans are roasted and ground.

_____ 20. The whitish or yellowish fat that is a natural component of cocoa beans.

_____ 21. The finest or smoothest variety of confectioners' sugar.

_____ 22. The starchy inner portion of grain kernels.

_____ 23. The percentage of a grain kernel that is separated into a particular grade of flour.

_____ 24. Various enzymes, found in flour and in some malts, that convert starch into sugar.

_____ 25. A fine quality of wheat flour that is milled from the inner portions of the endosperm.

_____	26. A weak flour with a soft, smooth texture and a pure white color.
_____	27. Wheat flour to which bran flakes have been added.
_____	28. A mixture of rye flour and strong wheat flour.
_____	29. Cocoa that has been processed with an alkali.
_____	30. A mixture of finely ground almonds and sugar.
_____	31. A soft shortening with special additives that make it possible to blend the shortening with larger quantities of sugar and liquid than is possible with regular shortenings.
_____	32. The dry powder that results when natural fats are separated from roasted, ground cocoa beans.
_____	33. A water-soluble protein extracted from animal tissue, used as a jelling agent.
_____	34. A water-soluble plant fiber used as a jelling agent.
_____	35. A simple sugar available in the form of a clear, colorless, tasteless syrup.
_____	36. French term used for high-quality natural sweetened chocolate, containing no added fats other than cocoa butter.
_____	37. A slightly aged, cultured heavy cream.
_____	38. The mineral content of flour.
_____	39. The amount of water that a given flour can take up to form a dough of a standard consistency, expressed as a percentage of the weight of the flour.
_____	40. A type of yeast used for sweet doughs because it is better able to grow in the presence of high sugar concentrations.

B. FLOUR REVIEW

Briefly describe, using your own words, the *break system* for milling flour. Explain the term *extraction* as it relates to milling different grades of flour.

_____

_____

_____

_____

_____

Flour is the most important ingredient in the bakeshop, so it is necessary to familiarize yourself with the different types of flour available. Define or describe each of the following products. If the product is a wheat flour, indicate whether it is a strong or weak flour.

1. Straight flour: _____

_____

_____

2. Patent flour: _____

_____

_____

3. Bread flour: _____

_____

_____

4. Clear flour: _____

_____

_____

5. Cake flour: _____

_____

_____

6. Pastry flour: _____

_____

_____

7. Whole wheat flour: _____

_____

_____

8. Bran flour: _____

_____

_____

9. Rye flour: _____

_____

_____

10. Rye meal: _____

_____

_____

11. Rye blend: _____

_____

_____

C. SHORT-ANSWER QUESTIONS

1. List five functions of fats in baked goods.

   (a) _____

   (b) _____

   (c) _____

   (d) _____

   (e) _____

2. Why are pastry doughs made with butter often more difficult to handle than those made with shortening? _____

   _____

   _____

3. What are two advantages of using butter instead of shortening in a pastry dough?

   _____

   _____

4. List eight functions of eggs in baked products.

   (a) _____

   (b) _____

   (c) _____

   (d) _____

   (e) _____

   (f) _____

   (g) _____

   (h) _____

5.	Describe two ways of incorporating air into batters to provide leavening.

(a) _____

_____

(b) _____

_____

6.	At what temperatures does yeast grow best? _____

At what temperature is yeast killed? _____

7.	What are three functions of salt in baked goods?

(a) _____

(b) _____

(b) _____

8.	Why does devil's food cake have a reddish color? _____

_____

9.	Describe, in three general steps, how unflavored gelatin is incorporated into a recipe.

(a) _____

(b) _____

(b) _____

## D.	BAKESHOP MATH (U.S. Measures)

1.	A formula for biscuits requires 1 lb 8 oz skim milk and is leavened with 2 oz baking powder. A baker wishes to substitute buttermilk for the skim milk. How should the leavening be adjusted to compensate for the buttermilk? (Give exact quantities.)

_____

_____

2.	A formula for muffins requires 6 pints skim milk and is leavened with 7 oz baking powder. A baker wishes to substitute buttermilk for the skim milk. How should the leavening be adjusted to compensate for the buttermilk? (Give exact quantities.)

_____

_____

3. A quick bread recipe requires 2 lb buttermilk and is leavened with 1.25 oz baking soda. A baker wishes to substitute skim milk for the buttermilk. How should the leavening be adjusted? _____

    _____

4. A formula requires 1 lb 12 oz bitter (unsweetened) chocolate and 2 lb 8 oz shortening. A baker wishes to substitute natural cocoa powder for the chocolate.

    How much cocoa should be used? _____.

    How much shortening should be used? _____.

5. A formula requires 12 oz cocoa powder and 1 lb 4 oz shortening. A baker wishes to substitute unsweetened chocolate for the cocoa.

    How much chocolate should be used? _____.

    How much shortening should be used? _____.

E.   BAKESHOP MATH (Metric Measures)

1. A formula for biscuits requires 750 g skim milk and is leavened with 60 g baking powder. A baker wishes to substitute buttermilk for the skim milk. How should the leavening be adjusted to compensate for the buttermilk? (Give exact quantities.)

    _____

    _____

2. A formula for muffins requires 3 L skim milk and is leavened with 210 g baking powder. A baker wishes to substitute buttermilk for the skim milk. How should the leavening be adjusted to compensate for the buttermilk? (Give exact quantities.)

    _____

    _____

3. A quick bread recipe requires 1 kg buttermilk and is leavened with 40 g baking soda. A baker wishes to substitute skim milk for the buttermilk. How should the leavening be adjusted? _____

    _____

4. A formula requires 850 g bitter (unsweetened) chocolate and 1200 g shortening. A baker wishes to substitute natural cocoa powder for the chocolate.

    How much cocoa should be used? _____.

    How much shortening should be used? _____.

5. A formula requires 350 g cocoa powder and 580 g shortening. A baker wishes to substitute unsweetened chocolate for the cocoa.

    How much chocolate should be used? _____.

    How much shortening should be used? _____.

Chapter 5
Basic Baking Principles

This chapter provides an introduction to bakeshop production. It is important to fully understand the information it contains, because it lays the groundwork for all of your work in the bakeshop.

Gluten is the foundation of the structure of most baked goods made from doughs and batters. In this chapter you will read about the factors that affect development of gluten. In addition, you will learn about the changes that take place in a dough or batter as it is baked.

After studying Chapter 5, you should be able to:

1. Explain the factors that control the development of gluten in baked products.

2. Explain the changes that take place in a dough or batter as it bakes.

3. Prevent or retard the staling of baked items.

A.   TERMS

Fill in each blank with the term that is defined or described.

_____ 1. The interior of a baked dough product, excluding the crust.

_____ 2. An elastic substance made up of proteins in wheat flour.

_____ 3. The process by which proteins become firm, usually when heated.

_____ 4. The two proteins that make up the elastic substance described in number 2.

_____

_____ 5. The process of allowing stretched gluten fibers in mixed dough to adjust to their new length.

_____ 6. The process of absorbing water.

_____ 7. A measure of the acidity or alkalinity of a substance.

_____ 8. A browning process that occurs when proteins and sugars together are subjected to high heat.

_____ 9. A dough at the ideal state of development in the mixing process.

_____ 10. The process by which sugars brown when heated; this process plus the process described in number 8 are responsible for the browning of the crusts of baked goods.

_____ 11. The change in texture and aroma of baked goods resulting from the loss of moisture from the starch granules.

_____ 12. Flour with a high protein content.

_____ 13. Any fat used in baking to tenderize a product by shortening gluten strands.

_____ 14. Flour with a low protein content.

_____ 15. The process by which starch granules absorb water and swell in size.

_____ 16. The gas released by the action of yeast and by baking powder and baking soda.

_____ 17. The production or incorporation of gases, followed by the expansion of these gases, in a baked product, that increases the volume of the product and changes its texture.

B. SHORT-ANSWER QUESTIONS

Fill in the blanks as required.

1. What are seven factors that affect how much gluten will be developed in a dough or batter?

    (a) _____

    (b) _____

    (c) _____

    (d) _____

    (e) _____

    (f) _____

    (g) _____

2. The three phases of mixing in the production of doughs and batters are:

    (a) _____

    (b) _____

    (c) _____

3. A cookie or pastry that is very crumbly due to high _____ content and little _____ development is said to be "short."

4. Two factors that cause baked goods to become stale are loss of _____ and a chemical change in starch structure called _____

    _____.

5. Loss of crispness is caused by the absorption of _____.

6. List three ways to slow the staling of baked goods.

    (a) _____

    (b) _____

    (c) _____

7. List the seven stages of the baking process.

    (a) _____

    (b) _____

    (c) _____

    (d) _____

    (e) _____

    (f) _____

    (g) _____

8. Why is ice water usually used to mix pie dough?

    _____

    _____

    _____

9. Describe the function and importance of the air cells that are formed in a dough or batter when it is mixed.

    _____

    _____

    _____

    _____

10. Describe the effects of oxidation on yeast doughs. How can oxidation be controlled?

_____

_____

_____

_____

11. The proteins from what kind of flour form the best-quality, strong, elastic gluten?

_____

Chapter 6

Understanding Yeast Doughs

Breads and other yeast goods are perhaps the most important products of the bakeshop. Breads are a large area of study, so the subject matter is divided into four chapters. This chapter discusses procedures for making breads and other yeast products. Special emphasis is placed on various types of dough-making processes and on controlling fermentation. Chapter 7 introduces more advanced subject matter related to artisanal breads. Specific formulas and makeup techniques are included in Chapters 8 and 9.

After studying Chapter 6, you should be able to:

1. List and describe the 12 basic steps in the production of yeast goods.

2. Explain the three basic mixing methods used for yeast doughs.

3. Explain the three basic techniques for developing yeast doughs, based on mixing times and speeds.

4. Describe the principal types of straight dough processes and list the advantages of sponge processes.

5. Understand and control the factors affecting dough fermentation.

6. Recognize and correct faults in yeast products.

A.   TERMS

Fill in each blank with the term that is defined or described.

_____   1.   A method of deflating dough to expel carbon dioxide and develop gluten during or after bulk fermentation.

_____   2.   A dough that is low in fat and sugar.

_____   3.   A dough that is high in fat, sugar, and sometimes eggs.

_____   4.   The rapid rise of a yeast dough in the oven due to the production and expansion of gases.

_____   5.   The process by which yeast acts on carbohydrates to produce alcohol and carbon dioxide.

31

_____   6. A dough that has not fermented long enough.

_____   7. A term describing a yeast dough that is easily stretched,

_____   8. Refrigerating a yeast dough to slow the fermentation.

_____   9. A bread dough that is made with a large quantity of yeast and given no fermentation time except for a short rest after mixing.

_____   10. The process of shaping scaled dough into smooth, round balls.

_____   11. A term describing a yeast dough that springs back when stretched.

_____   12. A dough in which fat is incorporated into the dough in many layers using a folding and rolling procedure.

_____   13. A liquid that is brushed onto the surface of a product, usually before baking.

_____   14. A mixing technique requiring a short mixing time and a long fermentation time.

_____   15. A bread that is baked directly on the bottom of the oven, not in a pan.

_____   16. A yeast dough mixing method in which all ingredients are combined at once.

_____   17. A mixing technique requiring a long mixing time and a short fermentation time.

_____   18. A yeast dough mixing method in which flour and other ingredients are mixed into a yeast batter or dough that has already had some fermentation time.

_____   19. The continuation of the yeast action, as described in number 6, after the dough has been shaped into loaves or other products, resulting in an increase in volume.

_____   20. A machine that can be set to retard dough and then automatically to begin proofing the dough at a preset time.

_____   21. A mixing technique requiring a medium mixing time and a medium fermentation time.

_____   22. Making cuts on the surface of proofed breads to improve their appearance and to help them rise better in the oven.

_____   23. A term describing a dough that is difficult to stretch.

B. TRUE OR FALSE

T	F	1.	Hard-crusted breads, such as French bread, should not be wrapped.
T	F	2.	High butter content in a yeast dough encourages more rapid fermentation.
T	F	3.	Overmixing is never a problem with lean bread doughs because of their strong gluten content.
T	F	4.	Baking with steam helps to form a thick crust on French bread.
T	F	5.	Dinner rolls should be proofed at about 75°F (24°C).
T	F	6.	Low humidity should be used for proofing hard rolls to keep them from forming soggy crusts.
T	F	7.	Hearth breads are baked with the seams on the bottom.
T	F	8.	Salt weakens gluten.
T	F	9.	The intensive mix technique gets its name from its long and intensive fermentation period.
T	F	10.	Short mix doughs need a long fermentation period because they are underdeveloped after mixing.
T	F	11.	Making a gluten window is a good way to test how well a dough has been mixed.
T	F	12.	Intensive mix doughs must be folded several times during fermentation.
T	F	13.	Proper preshaping makes final shaping or molding of loaves easier.
T	F	14.	The intensive mix technique is a good one to use for bagels because it results in the tight crumb that bagels require.
T	F	15.	If loaves are overproofed, they should be scored with deep cuts before baking.
T	F	16.	When calculating water temperature for yeast doughs, you should use a standard machine friction factor for all doughs in your bakeshop.

C.   YEAST DOUGH PRODUCTION

1.   List the 12 steps in the production of yeast goods.

1. _____   7. _____

2. _____   8. _____

3. _____   9. _____

4. _____   10. _____

5. _____   11. _____

6. _____   12. _____

2.   In the space provided, write the procedure for mixing yeast doughs by the straight dough method.

3.   In the space provided, write the procedure for mixing yeast doughs by the modified straight dough method. For what types of doughs is this method used? Why

4.   In the space provided, write the procedure for mixing yeast doughs by the sponge method.

D.   BAKESHOP MATH (U.S. Measures)

1.   A formula requiring 8 oz of yeast has a fermentation time of 90 minutes at 80°F. How much yeast is required if you want to increase the fermentation time to 2 hours?

_____

2.   A formula requiring 1 lb of yeast has a fermentation time of 2 hours at 80°F. How much yeast is required if you want to reduce the fermentation time to 90 minutes?

_____

3.   Given the following, factors, calculate the water temperature needed to make a mixed dough with a temperature of 80°F.

Flour temperature	=	74°F
Room temperature	=	75°F
Machine friction	=	20°F
Water temperature	=	_____

4.   Given the following factors, calculate the water temperature needed to make a mixed dough with a temperature of 75°F.

Flour temperature	=	70°F
Room temperature	=	73°F
Machine friction	=	20°F
Water temperature	=	_____

E. BAKESHOP MATH (Metric Measures)

1. A formula requiring 250 g yeast has a fermentation time of 90 minutes at 27°C. How much yeast is required if you want to increase the fermentation time to 2 hours?

    _____

2. A formula requiring 450 g yeast has a fermentation time of 2 hours at 27°C. How much yeast is required if you want to reduce the fermentation time to 90 minutes?

    _____

3. Given the following, factors, calculate the water temperature needed to make a mixed dough with a temperature of 26°C.

    Flour temperature   =   23°C

    Room temperature   =   24°C

    Water temperature   =   _____

4. Given the following factors, calculate the water temperature needed to make a mixed dough with a temperature of 24°C.

    Flour temperature   =   21°C

    Room temperature   =   23°C

    Machine friction   =   11°C

    Water temperature   =   _____

Chapter 7

Understanding Artisan Breads

Chapter 6 introduced you to the basic techniques and procedures for making a wide variety of breads and other yeast dough products. This chapter explains additional concepts and techniques that you must understand before producing more complex breads, including breads made with sourdough starters and yeast pre-ferments. After mastering the material in this chapter, you should be able to use the sourdough and other specialty formulas in Chapter 8.

After studying Chapter 7, you should be able to:

1. Select flour for making artisan breads.

2. Prepare yeast pre-ferments.

3. Prepare and maintain a sourdough starter.

4. Mix bread doughs using the technique called autolyse.

5. Bake artisan breads properly.

A.   TERMS

Fill in each blank with the term that is defined or described.

_____	1.	A handmade bread made according to traditional methods, without chemical additives, and with pre-ferments.
_____	2.	French term for sourdough starter.
_____	3.	The type of bacteria most common in sourdough starters.
_____	4.	A yeast pre-ferment made of equal weights of flour and water.
_____	5.	Italian term for a stiff yeast pre-ferment.
_____	6.	The process of hydrating flour before mixing with yeast and salt.
_____	7.	French term for yeast pre-ferment.
_____	8.	A dough leavened by a sourdough starter.

_____ 9. A fermented dough that is used to leaven a larger batch of dough.

_____ 10. French term for yeast.

_____ 11. A thin or wet sourdough starter.

_____ 12. French term for scrap dough.

B.   TRUE OR FALSE

T   F   1.   Biga and poolish are two types of yeast pre-ferment.

T   F   2.   Most breads referred to as "artisan" are hearth breads.

T   F   3.   Barm and pâte fermentée are two types of sourdough starter.

T   F   4.   In order to be called "artisan," a bread must contain no ingredients other than flour, water, salt, and yeast.

T   F   5.   The purpose of autolyse is to give the yeast a head start so that fermentation will be faster.

T   F   6.   Artisan breads are generally fermented at a lower temperature than typical commercially made breads.

T   F   7.   European-style breads use stronger flours than typical North American breads.

T   F   8.   High-extraction flour usually is darker in color than patent flour.

T   F   9.   Mixed fermentation refers to the use of both a pre-ferment and additional yeast to ferment a dough.

T   F   10. A thin or wet sourdough starter is more stable than a stiff, dough-like starter.

T   F   11. Stiff sourdough starters produce more acetic acid than more liquid starters.

T   F   12. When a yeast pre-ferment is being mixed, the gluten should be well developed.

T   F   13. When making a poolish, enough yeast should be used so that the fermentation time is short.

T   F   14. Sourdough starter should always be refreshed before using in a bread dough.

T   F   15. Yeast pre-ferments should be refreshed and stored like sourdough starters.

T   F   16. Yeast is very active in a poolish because of its high water content.

C. SOURDOUGH PRODUCTION

In the space below, write the procedure for making a sourdough starter.

Chapter 8

Lean Yeast Doughs

The general procedures and theories discussed in Chapter 6 and 7 are applied to specific formulas and makeup techniques for lean dough products in this chapter. As you mix, shape, pan, and bake the products discussed here, review the explanations and procedures in Chapter 6 and 7, as necessary.

After studying Chapter 8, you should be able to:

1. Prepare lean straight doughs and doughs made with a sponge or pre-ferment.

2. Prepare natural starters and yeast starters, and mix sourdoughs using them.

3. Make up a variety of loaf and roll types using lean doughs.

4. Prepare a variety of specialty bread items with nonstandard makeup and baking techniques, including English muffins, crumpets, and bagels.

A.   TERMS

Fill in each blank with the term that is defined or described.

_____ 1.   A coarse, heavy bread made with rye meal.

_____ 2.   A rectangular loaf made in a pan with a lid.

_____ 3.   A yeast dough made with a sponge or starter that has fermented so long that it has become very acidic or sour.

_____ 4.   A scaled unit of dough to be put into a dough divider.

_____ 5.   A French regional bread made in the shape of a trellis or ladder.

_____ 6.   A ring-shaped lean yeast dough product made from a very stiff dough.

_____ 7.   A disk-shaped yeast product made from a soft dough and cooked on a griddle.

_____ 8.   A disk-shaped yeast product made from a batter and cooked in a metal ring on a griddle.

_____ 9.   A type of Italian yeast bread made from a slack dough deposited on pans with minimal shaping.

_____ 10. An Italian flat bread similar to a thick pizza dough.

41

_____ 11. French name for country-style bread.

_____ 12. A quantity of grains that have been soaked in water to hydrate them before incorporating them in a bread dough.

B.   TRUE OR FALSE

T   F   1.   French breads always contain shortening, whereas the fat used in Italian bread is olive oil.

T   F   2.   French bread is given a very short proof in order to create the characteristic dense texture.

T   F   3.   Bagels are boiled before baking.

T   F   4.   Sour doughs are somewhat difficult to handle because they are generally stickier than regular bread doughs.

T   F   5.   One standard press makes 25 rolls.

T   F   6.   Ciabatta is made with a stiff dough.

T   F   7.   Yeast starters take longer to develop than natural starters.

T   F   8.   Sour starters are maintained by adding more flour and water to them each day in the same proportion as the original formula.

T   F   9.   Sourdoughs containing a high proportion of sour are usually underproofed.

T   F   10. Soft pretzels are dipped in a baking soda solution before being baked.

C.   USING BAKER'S PERCENTAGES

Use the percentages given to calculate the quantities needed in the following formulas. (You are provided with either the weight of the flour or the total yield by weight.) Fill in the blanks with your answers. Do either the U.S. or metric calculations or both, as directed by your instructor.

I.

	U.S. Measures	Baker's %	Metric Measures
Water	_____	62%	_____
Yeast, fresh	_____	4%	_____
Bread flour	4 lb	100%	21 g
Salt	_____	2%	_____
Sugar	_____	4	_____

II.

	U.S. Measures	Baker's %	Metric Measures
Bread flour	_____	100%	_____
Sugar	_____	10%	_____
Salt	_____	2%	_____
Yeast, fresh	_____	3%	_____
Eggs	_____	10%	_____
Milk	_____	50%	_____
Butter	_____	15%	_____
Malt syrup	_____	1%	_____
Yield:	7 lb	191%	3400 g

D. CALCULATING FORMULA COSTS

Cost out the following formula. For the prices of ingredients, use figures supplied by your instructor or taken from the Appendix, "Sample Prices," in this Study Guide. The problem is given in both U.S. and metric measures. Complete the problem assigned by your instructor.

Item: Soft Rolls

Yield: 9 lb 14 oz

Ingredients	Amount	Amount in Converted Units	EP Unit Cost ($)	Total ($)
Water	3 lb 2 oz	_____	_____	_____
Yeast, fresh	3 oz	_____	_____	_____
Bread flour	5 lb 4 oz	_____	_____	_____
Salt	1.5 oz	_____	_____	_____
Sugar	8 oz	_____	_____	_____
Nonfat milk solids	4 oz	_____	_____	_____
Shortening	4 oz	_____	_____	_____
Butter	4 oz	_____	_____	_____
Total cost				_____
Quantity produced				_____
Cost per lb				_____

Item: Soft Rolls

Yield: 4740 g

Ingredients	Amount	Amount in Converted Units	EP Unit Cost ($)	Total ($)
Water	1500 g	_____	_____	_____
Yeast, fresh	90 g	_____	_____	_____
Bread flour	2500 g	_____	_____	_____
Salt	50 g	_____	_____	_____
Sugar	240 g	_____	_____	_____
Nonfat milk solids	120 g	_____	_____	_____
Shortening	120 g	_____	_____	_____
Butter	120 g	_____	_____	_____
Total cost				_____
Quantity produced				_____
Cost per kg				_____

Chapter 9
Rich Yeast Doughs

As in Chapter 8, the formulas and makeup techniques presented in this chapter are based on the general theories and procedures explained in Chapter 6. Review the procedures in Chapter 6 as necessary to enable you to make the doughs and perform the makeup techniques in this chapter.

Pay special attention to the rolling-in procedure for Danish and croissant doughs. This is an important technique to master. You will find that careful practice of this procedure will help you when you learn the slightly different rolling-in procedure for puff pastry, detailed in Chapter 14.

After studying Chapter 9, you should be able to:

1. Produce simple sweet doughs.

2. Produce laminated yeast doughs.

3. Prepare a variety of toppings and fillings for rich yeast doughs.

4. Make up a variety of products using sweet doughs and laminated doughs, including Danish pastry and croissants.

A. TERMS

Fill in each blank with the term that is defined or described.

_____ 1. Crumb topping for pastries, made of flour, butter, and sugar.

_____ 2. A crescent-shaped roll made with a rolled-in dough.

_____ 3. A dough in which fat is incorporated into the dough in many layers by using a folding and rolling procedure.

_____ 4. Another name for a type of sweet almond filling.

_____ 5. French name for a type of rich, flaky roll with a chocolate filling.

_____ 6. A fold used to make Danish dough, in which the dough is folded in thirds.

_____ 7. A rich yeast dough containing large amounts of eggs and butter, usually made into rolls with round topknots, and baked in fluted tins.

_____ 8. A type of yeast bread or cake that is soaked in syrup.

45

_____ 9. An Italian sweetbread made in a large, round loaf, usually containing dried and candied fruits.

_____ 10. A type of yeast recommended for doughs high in sugar.

B. TRUE OR FALSE

T   F   1.   Because the gluten is not as strong in sweet roll dough as it is in white bread dough, the sweet roll dough is given a fuller proof.

T   F   2.   The sponge method is often used for mixing sweet doughs.

T   F   3.   Croissants and brioche are two examples of rolled-in dough products.

T   F   4.   When a rich dough contains a high proportion of sugar, the sugar is often creamed with the fat so that it will be more evenly distributed in the dough.

T   F   5.   Sheet pans for baking sweet dough products should be greased heavily, as opposed to lining with silicone paper, to prevent the bottoms from burning.

T   F   6.   A kugelhopf is baked in a buttered tube pan.

T   F   7.   Croissant dough contains more eggs than Danish dough.

T   F   8.   After the butter is enclosed in Danish dough, the dough is given four simple folds, or turns.

T   F   9.   When most sweet dough products are iced with flat icing, the icing is drizzled over them; it doesn't cover them completely.

T   F   10. Bear claws, Danish spirals, and Danish pockets are all made up from filled dough rolls.

T   F   11. The intensive mix technique is recommended for laminated doughs in order to develop the gluten.

T   F   12. Danish dough products are best egg-washed both before and after proofing.

T   F   13. Laminated doughs should be proofed at 85°F (29°C).

T   F   14. Egg-washed products are baked with less steam than regular breads.

T   F   15. Danish dough products should be removed from sheet pans immediately after baking.

C.   USING BAKER'S PERCENTAGES

Use the percentages given to calculate the quantities needed in the following formulas. You are provided with either the weight of the flour or the total yield by weight. Fill in the blanks with your answers. Do either the U.S. or metric calculations or both as directed by your instructor.

I.	U.S. Measures	Baker's %	Metric Measures
Milk	_____	30%	_____
Yeast, fresh	_____	5%	_____
Bread flour	_____	33%	_____
Butter	_____	40%	_____
Sugar	_____	20%	_____
Salt	_____	1.25%	_____
Eggs	_____	37%	_____
Bread flour	_____	67%	_____
Raisins	_____	10%	_____
Yield:	4 lb 8 oz	243%	2190 g

II.

	U.S. Measures	Baker's %	Metric Measures
Milk	_____	16%	_____
Yeast, fresh	_____	5%	_____
Bread flour	10 oz	20%	300 g
Eggs	_____	54%	_____
Bread flour	2 lb 8 oz	80%	1200 g
Sugar	_____	5%	_____
Salt	_____	1.25%	_____
Butter	_____	70%	_____

D. CALCULATING FORMULA COSTS

Cost out the following formula. For the prices of ingredients, use figures supplied by your instructor or taken from the Appendix, "Sample Prices," in this Study Guide. The problem is given in both U.S. and metric measures. Complete the problem assigned by your instructor.

Item: Sweet Roll Dough

Yield: 10 lb 7 oz

Ingredients	Amount	Amount in Converted Units	EP Unit Cost ($)	Total ($)
Water	2 lb	_____	_____	_____
Yeast, fresh	6 oz	_____	_____	_____
Butter	1 lb	_____	_____	_____
Sugar	1 lb	_____	_____	_____
Salt	1.5 oz	_____	_____	_____
Nonfat milk solids	4 oz	_____	_____	_____
Eggs	12 oz	_____	_____	_____
Bread flour	4 lb	_____	_____	_____
Cake flour	1 lb	_____	_____	_____
		Total cost		_____
		Quantity produced		_____
		Cost per lb		_____

Item: Sweet Roll Dough

Yield: 4190 g

Ingredients	Amount	Amount in Converted Units	EP Unit Cost ($)	Total ($)
Water	800 g	_____	_____	_____
Yeast, fresh	150 g	_____	_____	_____
Butter	400 g	_____	_____	_____
Sugar	400 g	_____	_____	_____
Salt	40 g	_____	_____	_____
Nonfat milk solids	100 g	_____	_____	_____
Eggs	300 g	_____	_____	_____
Bread flour	1600 g	_____	_____	_____
Cake flour	400 g	_____	_____	_____
Total cost				_____
Quantity produced				_____
Cost per kg				_____

Chapter 10
Quick Breads

Although short, this chapter explains a number of important procedures used to prepare a variety of popular baked goods. These products also have the advantage of being relatively quick and easy to prepare.

After studying Chapter 10, you should be able to:

1. Prepare baking powder biscuits and variations of them.

2. Prepare muffins, quick loaf breads, coffee cakes, and cornbreads.

3. Prepare popovers.

A.   TERMS

Fill in each blank with the term that is defined or described.

_____   1.   A batter that is too thick to be poured, but will drop in lumps from a spoon.

_____   2.   A batter that is liquid enough to be poured.

_____   3.   A baked product made of a thin batter, leavened only by steam, and characterized by large holes or cavities on the inside.

_____   4.   The development of elongated holes inside muffin products.

B.   REVIEW OF MIXING METHODS

1.   In the space below, write the procedure for mixing dough by the biscuit method.

2.   In the space below, write the procedure for mixing batters by the muffin method.

3.   In the space below, write the procedure for mixing biscuit doughs by the creaming method.

4.   In the space below, write the procedure for mixing muffin batters by the creaming method.

C. USING BAKER'S PERCENTAGES

Use the percentages given to calculate the quantities needed in the following formulas. (You are provided with either the weight of the flour or the total yield by weight.) Fill in the blanks with your answers. Do either the U.S. or metric calculations or both, as directed by your instructor.

I.

	U.S. Measures	Baker's %	Metric Measures
Pastry flour	1 lb 11 oz	85%	765 g
Whole wheat flour	5 oz	15%	135 g
Sugar		35%	
Baking powder		6%	
Salt		1.5%	
Pecans		19%	
Eggs		40%	
Milk		60%	
Melted butter		32%	

II.

	U.S. Measures	Baker's %	Metric Measures
Milk		200%	
Eggs		125%	
Salt		2%	
Melted butter		13%	
Bread flour		100%	
Yield:	2 lb 12 oz	440%	1320 g

54

D. CALCULATING FORMULA COSTS

Cost out the following formula. For the prices of ingredients, use figures supplied by your instructor or taken from the Appendix, "Sample Prices," in this Study Guide. The problem is given in both U.S. and metric measures. Complete the problem assigned by your instructor.

Item: Biscuits

Yield: 10 lb 10 oz

Ingredients	Amount	Amount in Converted Units	EP Unit Cost ($)	Total ($)
Bread flour	2 lb 8 oz	_____	_____	_____
Pastry flour	2 lb 8 oz	_____	_____	_____
Salt	1.5 oz	_____	_____	_____
Sugar	4 oz	_____	_____	_____
Baking powder	5 oz	_____	_____	_____
Shortening, regular	1 lb 12 oz	_____	_____	_____
Whole milk	3 lb 4 oz	_____	_____	_____
		Total cost		_____
		Quantity produced		_____
		Cost per lb		_____

Item: Biscuits

Yield: 5152 g

Ingredients	Amount	Amount in Converted Units	EP Unit Cost ($)	Total ($)
Bread flour	1200 g	_____	_____	_____
Pastry flour	1200 g	_____	_____	_____
Salt	48 g	_____	_____	_____
Sugar	120 g	_____	_____	_____
Baking powder	145 g	_____	_____	_____
Shortening, regular	840 g	_____	_____	_____
Whole milk	1600 g	_____	_____	_____
		Total cost		_____
		Quantity produced		_____
		Cost per kg		_____

Chapter 11
Doughnuts, Fritters, Pancakes, and Waffles

Some of the techniques you have studied in earlier chapters, including yeast dough production and quick-bread mixing methods, are applied again in this chapter. It discusses a variety of flour-based products that are not baked in the oven.

After studying Chapter 11, you should be able to:

1. Prepare doughnuts.

2. Prepare other deep-fried desserts and pastries.

3. Prepare pancakes and waffles.

4. Prepare crêpes and crêpe desserts.

A.   TERMS

Fill in each blank with the term that is defined or described.

_____   1.   French term for a type of waffle, often made from a thinned-out éclair paste.

_____   2.   French term for a thin, unleavened pancake.

_____   3.   A dessert made from unleavened pancakes, flavored with orange juice and orange liqueur, often flamed.

_____   4.   Pieces of fruit or other food dipped in a batter and deep-fried.

_____   5.   A small piece of éclair paste, fried and served warm, usually with sugar and a sauce.

_____   6.   A doughnut made with éclair paste.

_____   7.   A shiny, transparent icing applied to doughnuts.

_____   8.   Another name (from the German) for a jelly-filled doughnut.

_____   9.   An Indian pastry made of deep-fried batter and soaked in flavored syrup.

B. SHORT-ANSWER QUESTIONS

1. Explain why careful control of fermentation times is important when making yeast-raised doughnuts.

   _____

   _____

   _____

2. What is the proper dough temperature for cake-type doughnuts?

   _____

3. Why does too low a frying temperature make doughnuts greasy?

   _____

   _____

4. List seven guidelines for the use and care of deep-frying fat.

   (a) _____

   (b) _____

   (c) _____

   (d) _____

   (e) _____

   (f) _____

   (g) _____

5. After dough for cake doughnuts has been rolled out and cut, what is the next step in the procedure before frying them? _____

6. When doughnuts are coated with confectioners' sugar, should they be warm or cooled? Why?

   _____

   _____

7. What is the usual mixing method for American-style pancakes? _____

   What are the three basic steps in this mixing procedure?

   (a) _____

   (b) _____

   (c) _____

8. Waffle batter is similar to pancake batter, except that formulas for waffles often call for separating the eggs and whipping the egg whites. What are two other general differences between waffle batter and pancake batter formulas?

_____

_____

9. How can you tell when to turn pancakes over to fry the other side?

_____

_____

10. Why should pancake batter leavened with baking soda be made as close as possible to cooking time?

_____

_____

11. Six suggestions for crêpe desserts are described on page 250 (Crêpes Normande, Banana Crêpes, and so on); in addition, four full recipes are included on pages 250-253. Invent two additional desserts made with crêpes. Give them names, and describe them in the space below.

C.   USING BAKER'S PERCENTAGES

Use the percentages given to calculate the quantities needed in the following formulas. (You are provided with either the weight of the flour or the total yield by weight.) Fill in the blanks with your answers. Do either the U.S. or metric calculations or both, as directed by your instructor.

I.

	U.S. Measures	Baker's %	Metric Measures
Water	_____	55%	_____
Yeast	_____	5%	_____
Shortening	_____	10%	_____
Sugar	_____	14%	_____
Salt	_____	2%	_____
Milk solids	_____	5%	_____
Eggs	_____	14%	_____
Bread flour	_____	100%	_____
Yield:	10 lb	205%	5000 g

II.

	U.S. Measures	Baker's %	Metric Measures
Pastry flour	1 lb	100%	500 g
Sugar	_____	6%	_____
Salt	_____	1.5%	_____
Baking powder	_____	1.5%	_____
Eggs	_____	50%	_____
Milk	_____	90%	_____
Oil	_____	6%	_____
Vanilla	_____	1%	_____

D. CALCULATING FORMULA COSTS

Cost out the following formula. For the prices of ingredients, use figures supplied by your instructor or taken from the Appendix, "Sample Prices," in this Study Guide. The problem is given in both U.S. and metric measures. Complete the problem assigned by your instructor.

Item: Fritter Batter

Yield: 5 lb 11 oz

Ingredients	Amount	Amount in Converted Units	EP Unit Cost ($)	Total ($)
Pastry flour	2 lb 4 oz	_____	_____	_____
Sugar	2 oz	_____	_____	_____
Salt	0.5 oz	_____	_____	_____
Baking powder	0.5 oz	_____	_____	_____
Eggs	1 lb 2 oz	_____	_____	_____
Milk	2 lb	_____	_____	_____
Oil	2 oz	_____	_____	_____
Vanilla extract	0.33 oz	_____	_____	_____
		Total cost		_____
		Quantity produced		_____
		Cost per lb		_____

Item: Fritter Batter

Yield: 2670 g

Ingredients	Amount	Amount in Converted Units	EP Unit Cost ($)	Total ($)
Pastry flour	1000 g	_____	_____	_____
Sugar	60 g	_____	_____	_____
Salt	15 g	_____	_____	_____
Baking powder	15 g	_____	_____	_____
Eggs	500 g	_____	_____	_____
Milk	900 g	_____	_____	_____
Oil	60 g	_____	_____	_____
Vanilla extract	10 g	_____	_____	_____
Total cost				_____
Quantity produced				_____
Cost per kg				_____

Chapter 12

Basic Syrups, Creams, and Sauces

The creams, icings, and sauces introduced in this chapter are fundamental preparations essential to a wide variety of pastries, cakes, and desserts. Learn the basic procedures well, because you will need them for the recipes not only in this chapter, but throughout the rest of the book.

After studying Chapter 12, you should be able to:

1. Cook sugar syrups to various stages of hardness.

2. Prepare whipped cream, meringues, custard sauces, and pastry cream variations.

3. Prepare dessert sauces.

A.   TERMS

Fill in each blank with the term that is defined or described.

_____   1.   A thick, white foam made of whipped egg whites and sugar.

_____   2.   A foam made by whipping a boiling syrup into whipped egg whites.

_____   3.   A thick custard sauce containing eggs and starch.

_____   4.   A syrup consisting of sucrose and water in various proportions.

_____   5.   A flavored sugar syrup used to flavor and moisten cakes and other desserts.

_____   6.   A rich cream made of chocolate and heavy cream.

_____   7.   The browning of sugars caused by heat.

_____   8.   A foamy sauce or dessert made of egg yolks whipped over heat with wine or liqueur.

_____   9.   A mixture of pastry cream and meringue with flavorings and a gelatin stabilizer.

_____   10.   A sauce made of milk and sugar, thickened with egg yolks and flavored with vanilla.

_____   11.   French term for a sauce made of puréed fruit or other food.

63

_____ 12. A mixture of pastry cream and whipped cream.

_____ 13. French name for sweetened, vanilla-flavored whipped cream.

_____ 14. Egg whites and sugar warmed, usually over hot water, and then whipped to a foam.

_____ 15. A unit of measure indicating the sugar concentration of a solution; 1 degree on this measurement scale indicates 1 percent sugar concentration.

_____ 16. A unit of measure indicating the specific gravity of a solution, often used to determine sugar concentration.

_____ 17. A tool for measuring the sugar concentration of a solution, consisting of a weighted glass tube marked off in units of measure.

B.   REVIEW OF SUGAR COOKING

1. A simple syrup consists of _____ pound(s) of _____ dissolved in 1 pint of water.

2. To make a dessert syrup, you add a(n) _____ to a simple syrup.

   Dessert syrups are used to _____

   _____.

3. When melted sugar is heated, it turns brown. This browned sugar is called _____.

4. As a syrup is boiled, the concentration of sugar becomes _____ and the temperature of the syrup gradually _____.

5. Sometimes an acid, such as _____ or
   _____ is added to a boiling syrup to invert some of the sugar.

   The purpose of doing this is to_____

   _____

   _____.

6. What type of sugar should be used for boiled syrups? _____.

7. Sugar syrup cooked to a hard crack stage will have a temperature of about _____.

   When this sugar is cooled, its texture will be _____

   _____.

8. The most accurate way to tell when a syrup has reached the hard ball stage is to

   _____.

9. When cooking syrups, why should you try to keep sugar from forming crystals on the sides of the pan? _____

_____

C.   REVIEW OF CREAMS, MERINGUES, AND CUSTARDS

1. Why should heavy cream be chilled before whipping? _____

_____

2. The first sign that cream is becoming overwhipped is a _____

_____ appearance. If it continues to be whipped after this stage, it will

_____.

3. To avoid overwhipping cream, stop beating as soon as the cream _____

_____.

4. To make a stable whipped cream, the best type of sugar to use for sweetening is

_____.

5. Whipped cream that is to be mixed with other ingredients should be slightly underwhipped, because _____

_____

_____.

6. Describe the three basic types of meringues:

(a) Common meringue _____

_____

_____

(b) Swiss meringue _____

_____

_____

(c) Italian meringue _____

_____

_____

7. Egg whites to be whipped should have no trace of yolk in them because _____

_____.

8. Bowls and beaters for whipping egg whites should be checked carefully, to be sure they are clean and free of grease, because _____

_____.

9. Properly whipped egg whites are _____ in appearance. As they are overwhipped they begin to look _____.

10. Cream of tartar is sometimes added to egg whites for whipping because

_____.

11. Egg whites to be whipped should not be chilled because _____

_____.

12. The basic ingredients of crème anglaise are _____,

_____, _____, and_____.

13. Crème anglaise should be cooked until it reaches a temperature of _____.

14. What happens if a crème anglaise is overcooked? _____

_____

15. The ingredient that allows pastry cream to be cooked to a higher temperature than crème anglaise is _____.

16. The thickening or binding ingredient in crème anglaise is _____.

The primary thickening ingredient in pastry cream is _____; in addition, pastry cream is also thickened with _____.

17. List four sanitation rules to observe when preparing pastry cream. Why is sanitation important when preparing pastry cream?

(a)_____

(b)_____

(c)_____

(d)_____

_____

18. In its simplest form, ganache is a mixture of _____ and

_____.

19. In the space below, write the procedure for preparing crème anglaise. Use numbered steps.

20. In the space below, write the procedure for preparing vanilla pastry cream. Use numbered steps.

D.   USING BAKER'S PERCENTAGES

Use the percentages given to calculate the quantities needed in the following formula. (Note that there is no flour in this formula; the percentages are based on the ingredients indicated.) Fill in the blanks with your answers. Do either the U.S. or metric calculations or both, as directed by your instructor.

I.

	U.S. Measures	Baker's % Chocolate at 100%	Metric Measures
Sweet chocolate	12 oz	100%	350 g
Butter		50%	
Egg yolks		33%	
Egg whites		75%	
Sugar		16%	

II.

	U.S. Measures	Baker's % Milk at 100%	Metric Measures
Milk	1 lb 4 oz	100%	600 g
Sugar		20%	
Egg yolks		16%	
Cake flour		5%	
Cornstarch		5%	

E. CALCULATING FORMULA COSTS

Cost out the following formula. For the prices of ingredients, use figures supplied by your instructor or taken from the Appendix, "Sample Prices," in this Study Guide. The problem is given in both U.S. and metric measures. Complete the problem assigned by your instructor.

Item: Pastry Cream

Yield: 4½ pt

Ingredients	Amount	Amount in Converted Units	EP Unit Cost ($)	Total ($)
Milk	2 qt	_____	_____	_____
Sugar	8 oz	_____	_____	_____
Egg yolks	6 oz	_____	_____	_____
Whole eggs	8 oz	_____	_____	_____
Cornstarch	5 oz	_____	_____	_____
Sugar	8 oz	_____	_____	_____
Butter	4 oz	_____	_____	_____
Vanilla extract	1 oz	_____	_____	_____
		Total cost		_____
		Quantity produced		_____
		Cost per pt		_____

Item: Pastry Cream

Yield: 2.25 L

Ingredients	Amount	Amount in Converted Units	EP Unit Cost ($)	Total ($)
Milk, whole	2 L	_____	_____	_____
Sugar	250 g	_____	_____	_____
Egg yolks	180 g	_____	_____	_____
Whole eggs	250 g	_____	_____	_____
Cornstarch	150 g	_____	_____	_____
Sugar	250 g	_____	_____	_____
Butter	120 g	_____	_____	_____
Vanilla extract	30 mL	_____	_____	_____
		Total cost		_____
		Quantity produced		_____
		Cost per L		_____

Chapter 13

Pies

In the first part of this chapter you learn how to make basic pie doughs and assemble and bake pies. In the second half of the chapter, you learn how to make various pie fillings. The review exercises here will help you study this material.

After studying Chapter 13, you should be able to:

1. Prepare pie doughs.

2. Roll pie doughs and line pie pans.

3. Fill, assemble, and bake single-crust pies, double-crust pies, and lattice-topped pies.

4. Form and bake pie shells for unbaked pies.

5. Prepare fruit fillings.

6. Prepare soft or custard-type pie fillings.

7. Prepare cream fillings.

8. Prepare chiffon fillings.

A.   TERMS

Fill in each blank with the term that is defined or described.

_____   1.   A light, fluffy pie filling containing whipped egg whites and, usually, gelatin.

_____   2.   A liquid that is thickened or set by the coagulation of egg protein.

_____   3.   An unbaked pie containing a pastry-cream-type filling.

_____   4.   A type of canned fruit with very little added water or juice.

_____   5.   A type of canned fruit with no added water.

_____   6.   Referring to canned fruit, the weight of the fruit without the juice.

_____   7.   A type of top crust made of strips of dough laid across each other or interwoven.

_____   8.   A type of starch that will thicken a liquid without being cooked.

B.   SHORT-ANSWER QUESTIONS

1.   The four basic ingredients of pie dough are _____, _____, _____, and _____.

2.   The two basic types of pie dough are _____ and _____.

3.   In the space below, write the "rubbed dough method" procedure for mixing the four ingredients listed in question 1 to make pie dough; use numbered steps. Be sure to explain the difference between the two types of dough named in question 2.

4.   If shortening is used to make pie dough, what type of shortening should be used?

_____

5.   The three basic ingredients of a crumb crust are _____, _____, and _____.

6.   Two basic types of baked pies are _____ and _____.

7.   Two basic types of unbaked pies are _____ and _____.

8.   After a fruit pie filling has been cooked, it should be _____ before filling the pie shell and baking.

9.   So that it will not form lumps, a starch must be mixed with _____ or _____ before being added to a hot liquid.

10.   Cream pies are thickened with _____.

11.   When rolling out pie dough, it is best to use as little flour as possible for dusting, because

_____.

12.   Fruit pies are baked at a _____ (high *or* low) temperature so that

_____

_____.

13.   The best type of pie dough to use for pumpkin pies is _____.

14.   The cooking method most often used to make pie fillings from canned fruit is the

_____.

15. The cooking method most often used to make pie fillings from fresh, raw fruit is the

_____.

16. Raw pineapple should not be mixed with gelatin because _____

_____.

C.   PIE FILLING PROCEDURE REVIEW

1. In the space below, explain how to make fruit pie fillings using the cooked fruit method. Write the procedure in the form of numbered steps.

2. In the space below, explain how to make fruit pie fillings using the cooked juice method. Write the procedure in the form of numbered steps.

3.	In the space below, write a general procedure for preparing chiffon pie fillings. Use numbered steps.

4.	In the space below, write the procedure for preparing lemon pie filling. Use numbered steps.

D. USING BAKER'S PERCENTAGES

Use the percentages given to calculate the quantities needed in the following formulas. (You are provided with either the weight of the flour or the total yield by weight.) Fill in the blanks with your answers. Do either the U.S. or metric calculations, or both, as directed by your instructor.

I.	U.S. Measures	Baker's %	Metric Measures
Pastry flour	_____	100%	_____
Shortening	_____	67%	_____
Water	_____	28%	_____
Salt	_____	1.5%	_____
Sugar	_____	4%	_____
Yield	5 lb	200%	2500 g

II.	U.S. Measures	Baker's %	Metric Measures
Pastry flour	2 lb	100%	900 g
Sugar	_____	17%	_____
Butter	_____	50%	_____
Egg yolks	_____	8%	_____
Water, cold	_____	25%	_____
Salt	_____	1%	_____

E. CALCULATING FORMULA COSTS

Cost out the following formula. For the prices of ingredients, use figures supplied by your instructor or taken from the Appendix, "Sample Prices," of this Study Guide. The problem is given in both U.S. and metric measures. Complete the problem assigned by your instructor.

Item: Fresh Apple Pie Filling

Yield: 12 lb

Ingredients	Amount	Amount in Converted Units	EP Unit Cost ($)	Total ($)
Apples, AP	13 lb 4 oz	_____	_____	_____
Butter	5 oz	_____	_____	_____
Sugar	15 oz	_____	_____	_____
Water	10 oz	_____	_____	_____
Cornstarch	5 oz	_____	_____	_____
Sugar	1 lb	_____	_____	_____
Salt	0.3 oz	_____	_____	_____
Cinnamon	0.3 oz	_____	_____	_____
Nutmeg	0.15 oz	_____	_____	_____
Lemon juice	2 oz	_____	_____	_____
Butter	1.25 oz	_____	_____	_____
		Total cost		_____
		Quantity produced		_____
		Cost per lb		_____

Item: Fresh Apple Pie Filling

Yield: 5300 g

Ingredients	Amount	Amount in Converted Units	EP Unit Cost ($)	Total ($)
Apples, AP	6000 g	_____	_____	_____
Butter	150 g	_____	_____	_____
Sugar	450 g	_____	_____	_____
Water	300 g	_____	_____	_____
Cornstarch	150 g	_____	_____	_____
Sugar	500 g	_____	_____	_____
Salt	5 g	_____	_____	_____
Cinnamon	10 g	_____	_____	_____
Nutmeg	5 g	_____	_____	_____
Lemon juice	60 g	_____	_____	_____
Butter	35 g	_____	_____	_____
		Total cost		_____
		Quantity produced		_____
		Cost per kg		_____

Chapter 14
Pastry Basics

Pastries, cakes, and breads are the fundamental products of the bakeshop. This chapter presents the most important types of pastry doughs, with the exception of pie doughs, which are covered in Chapter 13. You will learn to mix these doughs and to make various simple baked goods with them. In the next chapter, you will learn to use these doughs to make more elaborate pastries.

After studying Chapter 14, you should be able to:

1. Prepare pâte brisée and short pastries.

2. Prepare puff pastry dough, blitz puff pastry dough, and reversed puff pastry doughs, and make simple pastries from these doughs.

3. Prepare pâte à choux (éclair paste) and make simple pastries from it.

4. Prepare strudel dough, handle commercial phyllo (strudel) dough, and make pastries using either homemade or commercial dough.

5. Bake meringue and meringue-type sponges, and assemble simple desserts with these meringues.

A.   TERMS

Fill in each blank with the term that is defined or described.

_____   1.   General English term for a type of rich pastry dough, similar to cookie dough, made with butter, sugar, and eggs, and used for tart shells.

_____   2.   French name for éclair paste.

_____   3.   A crisp disk of baked meringue containing nuts.

_____   4.   A dessert made of crisp baked meringues and ice cream.

_____   5.   Tiny cream puffs, often filled with ice cream and served with chocolate syrup.

_____   6.   A dessert made of layers of puff pastry alternating with layers of pastry cream or other cream or filling.

_____   7.   A type of dough that is mixed like pie dough but rolled and folded like puff paste.

_____   8.   A tart of caramelized apples, baked with the pastry on top, then turned upside down for display and service.

_____   9.   A paper-thin dough or pastry used to make strudels and various Middle Eastern and Greek desserts.

79

_____ 10. French name for a type of rich pastry dough, similar to a pie dough made with egg.

_____ 11. A type of dough that is stretched until it is paper-thin.

_____ 12. French term meaning "sugared dough"; similar to the dough described in number 10 but with more sugar.

_____ 13. The name for the method used to mix the dough described in number 10.

_____ 14. French term meaning "sanded dough"; a rich, sweet dough that can be used for pastries or cookies.

B.   TRUE OR FALSE

T   F   1. Bread flour is the preferred flour for éclair paste.

T   F   2. Danish dough and puff pastry dough are both rolled-in doughs, but Danish dough is leavened with yeast, while puff pastry dough is not.

T   F   3. Puff pastry products are baked at low temperatures to prevent burning or scorching.

T   F   4. Touching the edges of cut puff pastry dough units before baking may cause the layers to stick together at the edges and rise unevenly when baked.

T   F   5. Butter to be rolled into puff paste must be well chilled and hard so that it will not ooze out of the dough.

T   F   6. Éclair paste should be deposited on well-greased pans for baking.

T   F   7. When éclair paste is mixed, the eggs should be added all at once.

T   F   8. Puff pastry, éclair paste, and popover batter all depend on the same leavening agent.

T   F   9. Strudel dough is mixed well to develop strong gluten.

T   F   10. Strudel dough should be chilled well before stretching.

T   F   11. Pâte sablée is a type of puff pastry dough that can be made more quickly than classic puff pastry.

T   F   12. Short dough can be considered a type of cookie dough.

T   F   13. The quantity of rolled-in fat used for puff pastry may vary from 50 to 100% of the weight of the flour.

T   F   14 Unlike Danish dough, which is given three-folds or simple turns, puff pastry dough is always given four-folds.

C. PROCEDURE REVIEW

1. In the space below, write the basic procedure for making éclair paste. Use numbered steps.

2. In the space below, write the basic procedure for making pâte brisée. Use numbered steps.

3. In the space below, write a basic procedure for making puff pastry, beginning with the mixed dough and the block of butter. You may use any of the procedures in the text or the one preferred by your instructor. Use numbered steps.

D. USING BAKER'S PERCENTAGES

Use the percentages given to calculate the quantities needed in the following formulas. (You are provided with either the weight of the flour or the total yield by weight.) Fill in the blanks with your answers. Do either the U.S. or metric calculations, or both, as directed by your instructor.

I.

	U.S. Measures	Baker's %	Metric Measures
Pastry flour	7 lb	100%	3200 g
Sugar		17%	
Butter		50%	
Egg yolks		8%	
Water		25%	
Salt		1%	

II.

	U.S. Measures	Baker's %	Metric Measures
Butter		67%	
Sugar		25%	
Salt		0.5%	
Eggs		20%	
Pastry flour		100%	
Yield:	5 lb	212%	2500 g

E.   CALCULATING FORMULA COSTS

Cost out the following formula. For the prices of ingredients, use figures supplied by your instructor or taken from the Appendix, "Sample Prices," of this Study Guide. The problem is given in both U.S. and metric measures. Complete the problem assigned by your instructor.

Item: Almond Short Dough

Yield: 7 lb 11 oz

Ingredients	Amount	Amount in Converted Units	EP Unit Cost ($)	Total ($)
Butter	2 lb	_____	_____	_____
Sugar	1 lb 8 oz	_____	_____	_____
Salt	0.4 oz	_____	_____	_____
Powdered almonds	1 lb 4 oz	_____	_____	_____
Eggs	6.5 oz	_____	_____	_____
Vanilla extract	0.2 oz	_____	_____	_____
Pastry flour	2 lb 8 oz	_____	_____	_____
		Total cost		_____
		Quantity produced		_____
		Cost per lb		_____

Item: Almond Short Dough

Yield: 3080 g

Ingredients	Amount	Amount in Converted Units	EP Unit Cost ($)	Total ($)
Butter	800 g	_____	_____	_____
Sugar	600 g	_____	_____	_____
Salt	10 g	_____	_____	_____
Powdered almonds	500 g	_____	_____	_____
Eggs	165 g	_____	_____	_____
Vanilla extract	5 g	_____	_____	_____
Pastry flour	1000 g	_____	_____	_____
		Total cost		_____
		Quantity produced		_____
		Cost per kg		_____

Chapter 15

Tarts and Special Pastries

This is the second of two chapters on pastry. Chapter 14 presents the most important pastry doughs and other preparations used in pastries. This chapter introduces you to a variety of tarts and then gives examples of other sophisticated pastries. These give you further practice using the doughs from Chapter 14 and offer the opportunity to develop your decorative skills.

After studying Chapter 15, you should be able to:

1. Prepare baked and unbaked tarts and tartlets.

2. Prepare a variety of special pastries based on puff pastry, choux pastry, and meringue-type pastry.

A. TERMS

Fill in each blank with the term that is defined or described.

_____ 1. A tart made of raspberry jam and a short dough containing nuts and spices.

_____ 2. A tart of caramelized apples, baked with the pastry on top and then turned upside down for display and service.

_____ 3. A dessert made of a ring of cream puffs set on a short dough base and filled with crème Chiboust or crème diplomat.

_____ 4. A pastry made of two layers of puff paste enclosing an almond filling.

_____ 5. A flat, baked item consisting of a pastry and a sweet or savory topping or filling; similar to a pie but usually thinner.

_____ 6. A dessert of the type described in number 5, with a filling of custard and prunes.

_____ 7. A southern Italian turnover pastry with a sweet cheese filling.

_____ 8. Any of a variety of small fancy cakes and other pastries, usually prepared in single-portion sizes.

85

B.   SHORT-ANSWER QUESTIONS

1.   Tart shells baked without a filling are docked before baking because

_____.

2.   Why is it important to select a dough with a good flavor when making tarts?

_____

_____

3.   The simplest kind of baked fruit tart consists of _____

_____.

4.   What is the purpose of sometimes spreading cake crumbs on the bottom of a tart shell before the fruit is added and the tart is baked?

_____

_____

5.   In the space below, write the procedure for making baked tart shells. Use numbered steps.

6.   If a fruit is too hard to be cooked completely when baked in a tart, what can you do to ensure that it will become tender? _____

_____

_____

7.   In the space below, write a procedure for making a simple, unbaked, fresh raspberry tart. Use numbered steps.

C. CALCULATING FORMULA COSTS

Cost out the following formula. For the prices of ingredients, use figures supplied by your instructor or taken from the Appendix, "Sample Prices" in this Study Guide. The problem is given in both U.S. and metric measures. Complete the problem assigned by your instructor.

Item: Financiers

Yield: 450 petits fours

Ingredients	Amount	Amount in Converted Units	EP Unit Cost ($)	Total ($)
Raisins	5 oz	_____	_____	_____
Rum	1 pt	_____	_____	_____
Cake flour	6.75 oz	_____	_____	_____
Confectioners' sugar	1 lb 4 oz	_____	_____	_____
Powdered almonds	6.75 oz	_____	_____	_____
Egg whites	13.5 oz	_____	_____	_____
Butter	13.5 oz	_____	_____	_____
Honey	10 oz	_____	_____	_____
		Total cost		_____
		Quantity produced		_____
		Cost per each		_____

Item: Financiers

Yield: 450 petits fours

Ingredients	Amount	Amount in Converted Units	EP Unit Cost ($)	Total ($)
Raisins	120 g	_____	_____	_____
Rum	475 mL	_____	_____	_____
Cake flour	195 g	_____	_____	_____
Confectioners' sugar	555 g	_____	_____	_____
Powdered almonds	195 g	_____	_____	_____
Egg whites	375 g	_____	_____	_____
Butter	375 g	_____	_____	_____
Honey	300 g	_____	_____	_____
		Total cost		_____
		Quantity produced		_____
		Cost per each		_____

Chapter 16

Cake Mixing and Baking

Cakes are among the most delicate products a baker makes, so it is important to mix and bake them with a great deal of precision and care. This chapter will help you study the mixing and baking methods for many types of cakes.

After studying Chapter 16, you should be able to:

1. Perform basic cake mixing methods.

2. Explain ingredient functions and the concepts behind formula balance.

3. Scale and bake cakes correctly.

4. Correct cake failures or defects.

5. Adjust formulas for baking at high altitudes.

6. Produce high-fat or shortened cakes, including high-ratio cakes and cakes mixed by creaming.

7. Produce foam-type cakes, including sponge, angel food, and chiffon cakes.

A. TERMS

Fill in each blank with the term that is defined or described.

_____	1.	A type of cake based on an egg-white foam and containing no fat.
_____	2.	A cake made of equal parts butter, sugar, flour, and eggs.
_____	3.	A general term for cakes made with whole-egg foams or egg-yolk foams.
_____	4.	A cake made of a whole-egg-and-sugar foam, flour, and sometimes melted butter, but no other liquid.
_____	5.	A type of cake made with an egg-white foam and oil.
_____	6.	A uniform mixture of two unmixable substances.
_____	7.	A cake-mixing method that begins with the blending of fat and sugar.
_____	8.	A cake-mixing method that requires the use of emulsified shortening.

_____   9.   A cake made by adding one thin layer of batter at a time to a pan and browning under a broiler or salamander.

_____   10.   A thin cake layer decorated with a baked-in design made with stencil paste.

B.   SHORT-ANSWER QUESTIONS

1.   If shortening is used to make old-fashioned pound cake mixed by the creaming method, the correct shortening to use is _____.

2.   Ingredients for a high-fat or shortened cake should be at _____ temperature for mixing.

3.   The term _high-ratio_, when applied to cakes, means that the weight of the

_____ in the formula is greater than the weight of the

_____.

4.   List five factors that can cause curdling or separation of ingredients when mixing high-fat cakes.

(a) _____

(b) _____

(c) _____

(d) _____

(e) _____

5.   Overmixing is likely to make a cake's texture _____ because of gluten development.

6.   Most cakes are made with _____ (strong _or_ weak) flour.

7.   Proper mixing speed for two-stage cakes is _____.

8.   The two-stage method gets its name because the _____ ingredients are added in two stages.

9.   The primary leavening agent for genoise is _____.

10.   Describe the texture of egg whites that have been properly whipped for angel food cake.

_____

11.   For the purpose of balancing cake formulas, ingredients can be classified according to four functions: _____, _____,

_____, and _____.

12. In the spaces following each of the ingredients below, write the name(s) of the functions that ingredient fills. Use the four functions that you listed in question 11. (Note that an ingredient may fill more than one function.)

Flour: _____

Sugar: _____

Eggs: _____

Water: _____

Liquid milk: _____

Nonfat milk solids: _____

Butter: _____

Shortening: _____

Baking powder: _____

Cocoa powder: _____

13. List three ways to determine when a high-fat cake is done baking.

(a) _____

(b) _____

(c) _____

C.   REVIEW OF CAKE-MIXING METHODS

1.   In the space below, write a procedure for mixing cakes by the creaming method. Use numbered steps.

2.   In the space below, write a procedure for mixing cakes by the two-stage method. Use numbered steps.

3. In the space below, write a procedure for mixing cakes by the one-stage (liquid shortening) method.

4. In the space below, write a procedure for mixing genoise cakes. Use numbered steps.

5.   In the space below, write a procedure for mixing angel food cakes. Use numbered steps.

6.   In the space below, write a procedure for mixing chiffon cakes. Use numbered steps.

D. USING BAKER'S PERCENTAGES

Use the percentages given to calculate the quantities needed in the following formulas. (You are provided with either the weight of the flour or the total yield by weight.) Fill in the blanks with your answers. Do either the U.S. or metric calculations, or both, as directed by your instructor.

I.	U.S. Measures	Baker's %	Metric Measures
Sugar	_____	95%	_____
Shortening	_____	20%	_____
Butter	_____	10%	_____
Salt	_____	1%	_____
Cinnamon	_____	0.5%	_____
Eggs	_____	20%	_____
Skim milk	_____	38%	_____
Cake flour	_____	100%	_____
Baking powder	_____	2.5%	_____
Baking soda	_____	2.5%	_____
Chopped apples	_____	100%	_____
Yield	5 lb	389%	2334 g

II.	U.S. Measures	Baker's %	Metric Measures
Sugar	_____	125%	_____
Whole eggs	_____	75%	_____
Egg yolks	_____	25%	_____
Salt	_____	1.5%	_____
Cake flour	2 lb 8 oz	100%	1200 g
Baking powder	_____	3%	_____
Skim milk	_____	50%	_____
Butter	_____	25%	_____
Vanilla	_____	3%	_____

E. CALCULATING FORMULA COSTS

Cost out the following formula. For the prices of ingredients, use figures supplied by your instructor or taken from the Appendix, "Sample Prices," in this Study Guide. The problem is given in both U.S. and metric measures. Complete the problem assigned by your instructor.

Item: Yellow Butter Cake

Yield: 13 lb 7 oz

Ingredients	Amount	Amount in Converted Units	EP Unit Cost ($)	Total ($)
Butter	2 lb 4 oz	_____	_____	_____
Sugar	3 lb	_____	_____	_____
Salt	0.5 oz	_____	_____	_____
Eggs	1 lb 11 oz	_____	_____	_____
Cake flour	3 lb 12 oz	_____	_____	_____
Baking powder	2.5 oz	_____	_____	_____
Milk, whole	2 lb 8 oz	_____	_____	_____
Vanilla extract	1 oz	_____	_____	_____
		Total cost		_____
		Quantity produced		_____
		Cost per lb		_____

Item: Yellow Butter Cake

Yield: 6477 g

Ingredients	Amount	Amount in Converted Units	EP Unit Cost ($)	Total ($)
Butter	1100 g	_____	_____	_____
Sugar	1450 g	_____	_____	_____
Salt	15 g	_____	_____	_____
Eggs	810 g	_____	_____	_____
Cake flour	1800 g	_____	_____	_____
Baking powder	72 g	_____	_____	_____
Milk, whole	1200 g	_____	_____	_____
Vanilla extract	30 g	_____	_____	_____
		Total cost		_____
		Quantity produced		_____
		Cost per kg		_____

Chapter 17

Assembling and Decorating Cakes

This chapter forms a unit with Chapters 16 and 18. Together, they explain the production, assembly, and decoration of a great variety of cakes. The chapter begins with a discussion of icings. It then proceeds to the basic procedures for assembling and icing the basic baked products, to make attractive desserts. The chapter also introduces some of the more artistic aspects of cake production. Careful practice and repetition, following your instructor's guidance, are essential to develop skills in these areas.

After studying Chapter 17, you should be able to:

1. Prepare icings.

2. Assemble and ice simple layer cakes, sheet cakes, and cupcakes.

3. Make and use a paper decorating cone.

4. Use a pastry bag to make simple icing decorations.

A.   TERMS

Fill in each blank with the term that is defined or described.

_____   1.   A form of icing made of confectioners' sugar and egg whites; used for decorating.

_____   2.   An icing made of butter and/or shortening blended with confectioners' sugar or sugar syrup, and sometimes other ingredients.

_____   3.   A mixture of confectioners' sugar and water, sometimes blended with other ingredients, used as an icing.

_____   4.   An icing made of meringue and gelatin.

_____   5.   A sugar syrup that is crystallized to a smooth, creamy white mass and used as an icing.

_____   6.   A sponge cake or other yellow cake filled with pastry cream and topped with chocolate fondant.

_____   7.   A pedestal with a flat, rotating top, used for holding cakes while they are being iced.

_____ 8. A plastic triangle with toothed or serrated edges, used for texturing icings.

_____ 9. A variety of small fancy cakes and other pastries, usually in single-portion sizes.

_____ 10. To partly mix two colors of icing to make a decorative pattern.

_____ 11. A transparent, sweet jelly used for decorating cakes.

B. REVIEW OF ICINGS

1. What are the three main functions of icings?

    (a) _____

    (b) _____

    (c) _____

2. For use, fondant should be heated to a temperature of _____.

    It should not be heated more than this because _____

    _____.

3. The two basic ingredients of simple buttercream are _____

    and _____.

4. Describe how to make decorator's buttercream. What is it used for?

    _____

    _____

    _____

    _____

5. In the space provided, use numbered steps to describe how to make French buttercream.

6. What is the difference between plain boiled icing and Italian meringue?

    _____

    _____

    _____

7. What is the difference between boiled icing and marshmallow icing?

_____

_____

_____

8. Describe how to make and store royal icing.

_____

_____

_____

_____

_____

9. Name three basic types of rolled coatings.

(a)_____

(b)_____

(c)_____

C.   REVIEW OF CAKE ASSEMBLY

1. What are the four basic components of a cake?

(a)_____

(b)_____

(c)_____

(d)_____

2. Each of the basic components of a cake, from question 1, has four characteristics that should be balanced and harmonized with one another to create an appealing cake. What are these four characteristics?

(a)_____

(b)_____

(c)_____

(d)_____

3. In the space below, use numbered steps to describe how to assemble and ice a simple American-style layer cake.

4. In the space below, use numbered steps to describe how to turn out, ice, and decorate a simple sheet cake with marked portions.

5. What does it mean to apply a masking layer of icing to a cake?

    What are the three advantages of this technique?

    (a)_____

    (b)_____

    (c) _____

6. Briefly describe each of the following decorating techniques:

(a) Stenciling: _____

_____

_____

(b) Marbling: _____

_____

_____

(c) Bowl knife patterns: _____

_____

_____

(d) Masking the sides of the cake: _____

_____

_____

(e) Piping jelly transfers: _____

_____

_____

D.   USING BAKER'S PERCENTAGES

Use the percentages given to calculate the quantities needed in the following formula. (Note that there is no flour in this formula; the percentages are based on the ingredients indicated.) Fill in the blanks with your answers. Do either the U.S. or metric calculations, or both, as directed by your instructor.

	U.S. Measures	Baker's % Sugar at 100%	Metric Measures
Sugar	1 lb 4 oz	100%	600 g
Water		25%	
Egg yolks		37.5%	
Butter		125%	
Vanilla		1.5%	

E. CALCULATING FORMULA COSTS

Cost out the following formula. For the prices of ingredients, use figures supplied by your instructor or taken from the Appendix, "Sample Prices," in this Study Guide. The problem is given in both U.S. and metric measures. Complete the problem assigned by your instructor.

Item: Caramel Fudge Icing

Yield: 8 lb

Ingredients	Amount	Amount in Converted Units	EP Unit Cost ($)	Total ($)
Brown sugar	6 lb	_____	_____	_____
Milk	3 pt	_____	_____	_____
Butter	1 lb 8 oz	_____	_____	_____
Salt	0.4 oz	_____	_____	_____
Vanilla extract	1 fl oz	_____	_____	_____
		Total cost		_____
		Quantity produced		_____
		Cost per lb		_____

Item: Caramel Fudge Icing

Yield: 4 kg

Ingredients	Amount	Amount in Converted Units	EP Unit Cost ($)	Total ($)
Brown sugar	3000 g	_____	_____	_____
Milk	1500 mL	_____	_____	_____
Butter	750 g	_____	_____	_____
Salt	8 g	_____	_____	_____
Vanilla extract	30 mL	_____	_____	_____
		Total cost		_____
		Quantity produced		_____
		Cost per kg		_____

Chapter 18
Specialty Cakes, Gâteaux, and Torten

This is the last of three chapters on cake baking, assembly, and decoration. Here you are introduced to more advanced techniques that will enable you to assemble elegant gâteaux and other specialty cakes. The photographs accompanying the many examples give you visual guidance as you learn to duplicate these creations.

After studying Chapter 18, you should be able to:

1. Select from a variety of components to plan cakes that have well-balanced flavors and textures.

2. Line charlotte rings or cake rings for specialty cakes.

3. Coat a cake with marzipan or rolled fondant.

4. Assemble a variety of European-style cakes, Swiss rolls, small cakes, and petits fours.

A.   TERMS

Fill in each blank with the term that is defined or described.

_____	1.	German word for various types of cakes, usually layer cakes.
_____	2.	A rich chocolate cake coated with apricot jam and chocolate fondant icing.
_____	3.	A small, bite-size, iced cake.
_____	4.	A layer cake iced and filled with coffee-flavored buttercream.
_____	5.	A thin sheet of sponge cake spread with a filling and rolled up.
_____	6.	French word for cake.
_____	7.	A chocolate sponge cake flavored with kirsch and filled with cherries and whipped cream.
_____	8.	A layer cake consisting of a top and bottom layer of baked meringue and a middle layer of sponge cake flavored with kirsch syrup.
_____	9.	A sponge layer cake iced with a macaroon mixture and then browned in the oven.

105

_____   10.   A cake made of seven thin layers, filled with chocolate buttercream, and topped with caramelized sugar.

_____   11.   A cake roll decorated to look like a log.

_____   12.   A type of small (single-portion size), spherical sponge cake filled with cream and iced with fondant.

_____   13.   A layer cake made of thin sponge layers, coffee-flavored buttercream, and chocolate ganache.

_____   14.   A metal ring used as a mold for charlottes and cakes.

B.   REVIEW OF CAKE ASSEMBLY

1.   In the space below, use numbered steps to describe how to assemble a basic layered sponge cake.

2. In the space below, use numbered steps to describe how to apply glaze to a cake.

3. In the space below, use numbered steps to describe how to line a ring mold with a sponge strip.

4. In the space below, use numbered steps to describe in detail how to assemble the following elements into a European-style layer cake.

    Base: chocolate meringue disk

    Cake: chocolate genoise, split into 2 layers

    Syrup: vanilla-flavored

    Filling: chocolate mousse

    Icing: chocolate buttercream

Chapter 19
Cookies

Learning to make cookies successfully and efficiently is mainly a matter of developing a number of manual skills. The portion of this chapter devoted to theory and basic principles is relatively short, but it contains important material that you should understand thoroughly. The questions here will help you review that material.

After studying Chapter 19, you should be able to:

1. Understand the causes of crispness, chewiness, and spread in cookies.

2. Prepare cookie doughs by the three basic methods.

3. Prepare eight basic types of cookies: dropped, bagged, rolled, molded, icebox, bar, sheet, and stencil.

4. Bake and cool cookies properly.

5. Prepare a variety of petits fours secs.

A. TERMS

Fill in each blank with the term that is defined or described.

_____ 1. A cookie made of coconut mixed with meringue.

_____ 2. An un-iced or unfilled petit four, such as a small butter cookie.

_____ 3. Cookies sliced from refrigerated, cylinder-shaped pieces of dough.

_____ 4. Cookies pressed from a pastry bag.

_____ 5. A rich Scottish cookie made of butter, flour, and sugar; some variations also contain egg.

_____ 6. Cookies made with a cookie cutter.

_____ 7. Cookies made from equal-size pieces of dough cut from a cylinder and then shaped.

_____ 8. Cookies made by spreading dough or batter on sheet pans, baking, and then cutting out squares or rectangles.

_____ 9. Finger-shaped soft cookies made from a sponge batter.

109

_____ 10. Readily absorbing moisture.

_____ 11. Cookies made from cylinders of dough placed on sheet pans, baked, then cut crosswise into pieces.

_____ 12. Cookies made from lumps of dough dropped onto baking pans.

_____ 13. A pattern cut from plastic or cardboard, used for depositing batter for thin cookies made in decorative shapes.

_____ 14. Crisp, Italian-style cookies made by the bar method and baked twice.

B.   SHORT-ANSWER QUESTIONS

1.   All the cookies in each batch should be made uniform in shape and size because

_____

_____.

2.   To prevent rich cookies from burning too easily on the bottom when baking, the baker can

_____

_____.

3.   What might happen to cookies that are cooled too rapidly?

_____

4.   Cookie doneness is indicated primarily by _____.

5.   Five factors that contribute to crispness in cookies are:

(a) _____

(b) _____

(c) _____

(d) _____

(e) _____

6.   Six factors that contribute to softness in cookies are:

(a) _____

(b) _____

(c) _____

(d) _____

(e) _____

(f) _____.

7. For each of the following items, indicate whether it increases or decreases a cookie's tendency to spread when baked.

    (a) High sugar content: _____

    (b) Using confectioners' sugar instead of granulated: _____

    (c) Low baking temperature: _____

    (d) Not greasing the baking sheet: _____

    (e) Excessive creaming: _____

    (f) High liquid content in batter: _____

    (g) Use of strong flour: _____

    (h) High baking powder content: _____

8. A cookie mixing method that begins with whipping eggs and sugar to a foam is a

    _____ method.

9. When cookies are rolled out with a rolling pin, no more flour than necessary should be used for dusting, because _____

    _____.

10. How does the egg content of a cookie mix affect the chewiness of the cookie?

    _____

    _____

C.   REVIEW OF COOKIE MIXING METHODS

1. Using numbered steps, describe the creaming method for mixing cookies.

2. Using numbered steps, describe the one-stage method for mixing cookies.

3. Using numbered steps, describe the sanding method for mixing cookies.

D.   USING BAKER'S PERCENTAGES

Use the percentages given to calculate the quantities needed in the following formulas. (You are provided with either the weight of the flour or the total yield by weight.) Fill in the blanks with your answers. Do either the U.S. or metric calculations, or both, as directed by your instructor.

I.	U.S. Measures	Baker's %	Metric Measures
Butter	_____	67%	_____
Brown sugar	_____	133%	_____
Salt	_____	1.5%	_____
Eggs	_____	33%	_____
Vanilla	_____	3%	_____
Milk	_____	8%	_____
Pastry flour	_____	100%	_____
Baking powder	_____	4%	_____
Baking soda	_____	2%	_____
Rolled oats	_____	83%	_____
Raisins	_____	67%	_____
Yield	11 lb	501%	5110 g

II.	U.S. Measures	Baker's %	Metric Measures
Butter	_____	90%	_____
Granulated sugar	_____	50%	_____
Confectioners' sugar	_____	40%	_____
Egg whites	_____	65%	_____
Vanilla	_____	1.5%	_____
Cake flour	1 lb 8 oz	75%	750 g
Bread flour	8 oz	25%	250 g

E. CALCULATING FORMULA COSTS

Cost out the following formula. For the prices of ingredients, use figures supplied by your instructor or taken from the Appendix, "Sample Prices," in this Study Guide. The problem is given in both U.S. and metric measures. Complete the problem assigned by your instructor.

Item: Spritz Cookies

Yield: 5 lb 12 oz

Ingredients	Amount	Amount in Converted Units	EP Unit Cost ($)	Total ($)
Almond paste	1 lb 8 oz	_____	_____	_____
Sugar	12 oz	_____	_____	_____
Salt	0.25 oz	_____	_____	_____
Butter	1 lb 8 oz	_____	_____	_____
Eggs	9 oz	_____	_____	_____
Vanilla extract	0.33 oz	_____	_____	_____
Cake flour	12 oz	_____	_____	_____
Bread flour	12 oz	_____	_____	_____
		Total cost		_____
		Quantity produced		_____
		Cost per lb		_____

Item: Spritz Cookies

Yield: 2948 g

Ingredients	Amount	Amount in Converted Units	EP Unit Cost ($)	Total ($)
Almond paste	750 g	_____	_____	_____
Sugar	375 g	_____	_____	_____
Salt	8 g	_____	_____	_____
Butter	750 g	_____	_____	_____
Eggs	290 g	_____	_____	_____
Vanilla extract	10 g	_____	_____	_____
Cake flour	375 g	_____	_____	_____
Bread flour	375 g	_____	_____	_____
Total cost				_____
Quantity produced				_____
Cost per kg				_____

Chapter 20

Custards, Puddings, Mousses, and Soufflés

This chapter presents a wide variety of techniques and products, but many of the preparations described here are based on techniques you have already learned. In particular, you should review the information on various custards and creams, in Chapter 12. These are fundamental techniques you should know well.

After studying Chapter 20, you should be able to:

1. Prepare starch-thickened or boiled puddings.

2. Prepare baked custards and baked puddings.

3. Prepare steamed puddings.

4. Prepare Bavarian creams and mousses.

5. Use Bavarian creams to prepare charlottes.

6. Prepare hot dessert soufflés.

A. TERMS

Fill in each blank with the term that is defined or described.

_____ 1. A soft or creamy dessert that is made light by the addition of whipped cream, egg whites, or both.

_____ 2. A baked dish containing whipped egg whites, which cause the dish to rise during baking.

_____ 3. A light, cold dessert made of gelatin, whipped cream, and crème anglaise or fruit.

_____ 4. A liquid that is thickened or set by the coagulation of egg protein.

_____ 5. An English boiled pudding made of milk, sugar, and cornstarch.

_____ 6. A custard baked in a mold lined with caramel, then unmolded.

117

_____ 7. A baked custard with a brittle top made of caramelized sugar.

_____ 8. A steamed pudding made of dried and candied fruits, spices, beef suet, and crumbs.

_____ 9. A cold dessert made of Bavarian or other cream in a special mold, usually lined with ladyfingers or another sponge product.

_____ 10. A rich baked custard served in a small cup.

_____ 11. A rich rice pudding containing whipped cream, candied fruits, and gelatin.

_____ 12. An Italian pudding made of cream, sugar, gelatin, and flavorings.

_____ 13. A type of pudding or cream consisting of crème anglaise plus additional binders or thickeners, including gelatin, butter, or chocolate.

B.   TRUE OR FALSE

T   F   1. Crème anglaise and baked custard are made of basically the same ingredients, but their cooking methods are different.

T   F   2. When scalded milk is added to egg yolks it should be added all at once.

T   F   3. Blancmange should not be heated to more than 185°F (85°C) during cooking.

T   F   4. Cream puddings, such as vanilla pudding, are prepared using the same procedure as for making pastry cream.

T   F   5. Butterscotch pudding is made by preparing vanilla pudding with extra butter and adding scotch flavoring.

T   F   6. Crème brûlée is usually richer than crème caramel because crème brûlée is made with heavy cream instead of milk.

T   F   7. Pumpkin pie filling and baked cheesecake are custards.

T   F   8. Bavarian creams are similar to mousses, but they are firmer because of their gelatin content.

T   F   9. If both whipped cream and whipped egg whites must be added to a chocolate mousse, the whipped cream is always added first.

T   F   10. An appropriate temperature for baking a soufflé is 375°F (190°C).

T   F   11. When chocolate is added to crémeux, the mixture is whipped until light.

C.   PROCEDURE REVIEW

1.   In the space below, write the procedure for making vanilla Bavarian cream. Use numbered steps.

2.   In the space below, write the procedure for making a simple baked custard. Use numbered steps.

3. In the space below, name the three basic components of a baked dessert soufflé. Explain each component, and give examples where appropriate.

4. In the space below, write the procedure for making vanilla-flavored panna cotta. Use numbered steps.

D. CALCULATING FORMULA COSTS

Cost out the following formula. For the prices of ingredients, use figures supplied by your instructor or taken from the Appendix, "Sample Prices," in this Study Guide. The problem is given in both U.S. and metric measures. Complete the problem assigned by your instructor.

Item: Chocolate Soufflé

Yield: 20 portions

Ingredients	Amount	Amount in Converted Units	EP Unit Cost ($)	Total ($)
Bread flour	6 oz	_____	_____	_____
Butter	6 oz	_____	_____	_____
Milk	1 qt	_____	_____	_____
Sugar	8 oz	_____	_____	_____
Unsweetened chocolate	6 oz	_____	_____	_____
Sweet, dark chocolate	2 oz	_____	_____	_____
Egg yolks	12 oz	_____	_____	_____
Vanilla extract	0.67 fl oz	_____	_____	_____
Egg whites	1 lb 4 oz	_____	_____	_____
Sugar	4 oz	_____	_____	_____
		Total cost		_____
		Quantity produced		_____
		Cost per portion		_____

121

Item: Chocolate Soufflé

Yield: 20 portions

Ingredients	Amount	Amount in Converted Units	EP Unit Cost ($)	Total ($)
Bread flour	180 g	_____	_____	_____
Butter	180 g	_____	_____	_____
Milk	1 L	_____	_____	_____
Sugar	240 g	_____	_____	_____
Unsweetened chocolate	180 g	_____	_____	_____
Sweet, dark chocolate	60 g	_____	_____	_____
Egg yolks	360 g	_____	_____	_____
Vanilla extract	20 mL	_____	_____	_____
Egg whites	600 g	_____	_____	_____
Sugar	120 g	_____	_____	_____
Total cost				_____
Quantity produced				_____
Cost per portion				_____

Chapter 21
Frozen Desserts

The frozen desserts, including ice creams, presented in this chapter use many of the same techniques as those introduced in previous chapters. For example, crème anglaise is the basis for ice cream and many frozen mousses, just as it is for the Bavarian creams in Chapter 20. And like Bavarian creams and mousses, still-frozen desserts depend on whipped cream or egg foams for their light texture. Thus, you might consider this chapter a continuation of Chapter 20.

After studying Chapter 21, you should be able to:

1. Judge the quality of commercial ice creams.

2. Prepare ice creams and sorbets.

3. Prepare ice cream and sorbet desserts using commercial or homemade ice creams and sorbets.

4. Prepare still-frozen desserts, including bombes, frozen mousses, and frozen soufflés.

A.   TERMS

Fill in each blank with the term that is defined or described.

_____   1.   A type of frozen dessert made in a dome-shaped mold and usually consisting of two or more layers.

_____   2.   The increase in volume of ice cream or frozen desserts caused by the incorporation of air while freezing.

_____   3.   A frozen dessert usually made of water, sugar, fruit juice or purée, and sometimes egg whites, milk, or cream.

_____   4.   A frozen dessert similar to that described in number 3, but with a coarse, crystalline texture.

_____   5.   A dessert consisting of a peach half and raspberry sauce on top of vanilla ice cream.

_____   6.   Ice cream made without eggs.

_____   7.   A frozen dessert similar to ice cream but made with milk and no cream.

_____   8.   A dessert consisting of one or two scoops of ice cream or sherbet served in a dish or glass and topped with any of a number of syrups, fruits, or toppings.

_____   9.   A dessert consisting of ice cream on a sponge cake base, covered with meringue and browned in the oven.

123

_____ 10. A dessert consisting of a pear half, chocolate sauce, and
                         toasted almonds over vanilla ice cream.

_____ 11. A dessert consisting of alternating layers of ice cream and
                         fruit or syrup in a tall, narrow glass.

_____ 12. A still-frozen dessert made in a tall, narrow mold.

B. SHORT-ANSWER QUESTIONS

1. What is overrun? How does it affect the quality of ice cream?

    _____

    _____

    _____

2. What are five factors that affect overrun?

    (a) _____

    (b) _____

    (c) _____

    (d) _____

    (e) _____

3. For storage, ice cream should be kept at a temperature of _____ or
    lower. For serving, it should be brought to a temperature of _____.

4. Why are careful sanitation procedures important when you are making ice cream?

    _____

    _____

    _____

5. When you are making sorbet, what information can you get by using a saccharometer?
    How is this information useful?

    _____

    _____

    _____

    _____

6. In the space below, write the procedure for making vanilla ice cream using egg yolks. Use numbered steps.

7. In the space below, write the procedure for making a frozen mousse with a meringue base. Use numbered steps.

8. In the space below, write the procedure for making a frozen mousse with a custard base. Use numbered steps.

C. CALCULATING FORMULA COSTS

Cost out the following formula. For the prices of ingredients, use figures supplied by your instructor or taken from the Appendix, "Sample Prices" in this Study Guide. The problem is given in both U.S. and metric measures. Complete the problem assigned by your instructor.

Item: Vanilla Ice Cream

Yield: 1 gal

Ingredients	Amount	Amount in Converted Units	EP Unit Cost ($)	Total ($)
Egg yolks	1 lb	_____	_____	_____
Sugar	1 lb 8 oz	_____	_____	_____
Milk	2 qt	_____	_____	_____
Heavy cream	1 qt	_____	_____	_____
Vanilla extract	0.67 fl oz	_____	_____	_____
Total cost				_____
Quantity produced				_____
Cost per qt				_____

Item: Vanilla Ice Cream

Yield: 4 L

Ingredients	Amount	Amount in Converted Units	EP Unit Cost ($)	Total ($)
Egg yolks	500 g	_____	_____	_____
Sugar	750 g	_____	_____	_____
Milk	2 L	_____	_____	_____
Heavy cream	1 L	_____	_____	_____
Vanilla extract	20 mL	_____	_____	_____
Total cost				_____
Quantity produced				_____
Cost per L				_____

Chapter 22
Fruit Desserts

Chapter 22 begins with a discussion of the characteristics, quality factors, and basic preparation procedures of fresh fruits—common fruits as well as exotic specialty varieties. The remainder of the chapter is devoted to the preparation of a selection of fruit desserts and various garnishes and condiments made of fruit.

After studying Chapter 22, you should be able to:

1. Select good-quality fresh fruits and prepare them for use in desserts.

2. Calculate fresh fruit yields based on trimming losses.

3. Prepare various fruit desserts, including poached fruits and fruit compotes.

A.   TERMS

Fill in each blank with the term that is defined or described.

_____	1.	A dish consisting of sweetened, sliced apples baked with a streusel or crumb topping.
_____	2.	Fresh or dried fruit poached in a syrup.
_____	3.	A dessert made of fruit baked with a pastry crust on top.
_____	4.	A dessert made by layering fruit and cake crumbs in a pan and then baking.
_____	5.	A hot dessert consisting of apples baked in a mold lined with buttered slices of bread.
_____	6.	French term for a colorless, nonsweet fruit brandy.
_____	7.	A sweet alcoholic beverage flavored with fruit, herbs, or other ingredients.
_____	8.	Term describing a fruit that is at its peak for texture and flavor and is ready to be eaten.
_____	9.	Term describing a fruit that has completed its development and is physiologically capable of continuing the ripening process.

B.   SHORT-ANSWER QUESTIONS

1.   List four fruits that will darken when cut and exposed to air.

    (a) _____

    (b) _____

    (c) _____

    (d) _____

    How can you prevent this browning? _____

    _____

2.   Describe in general terms how each of the following characteristics of fruits change as they become ripe:

    Aroma: _____

    _____

    Sweetness: _____

    _____

    Juiciness and texture: _____

    _____

    Color: _____

    _____

3.   The following statements describe the ripening characteristics of different fruits. For each description, list two fruits that have those characteristics.

    (a) These fruits are harvested fully ripe and do not ripen further after picking.

    _____, _____

    (b) These fruits do not become sweeter, but they do become juicier and softer, and their color changes when they ripen after picking.

    _____, _____

    (c) These fruits become sweeter, juicier, and softer, and their color changes when they ripen after picking.

    _____, _____

    (d) These fruits undergo changes in aroma, sweetness, juiciness, texture, and color when they ripen after picking.

    _____, _____

4. Why is it not advisable to refrigerate bananas? _____

5. Describe the best way to store, handle, and clean fresh raspberries. _____

    _____

6. What type of fruit dessert resembles a pie without a bottom crust? _____

7. Describe in general terms how to prepare a peach compote (poached peaches) for use as a dessert.

    _____

8. Peach crisp consists of sweetened sliced peaches baked with a topping of _____.

9. What piece of equipment is used to finish a fruit gratin before serving?

    _____

10. The thickening or binding agent used for jams and marmalades is _____.

C.   TRIMMING LOSS

The exercises below are of two kinds: calculating yield and calculating amount needed. To do the calculations, you need to know the percentage yield for each fruit, as listed in Chapter 22. For your convenience, the necessary percentages are repeated here.

Apples	75%
Apricots	94%
Cherries (pitted)	82%
Coconut	50%
Grapefruit (sections)	50%
Grapes	90%
Kiwi fruit	80%
Mangoes	75%
Watermelon	45%
Papaya	65%
Peaches	75%
Pineapple	50%
Plums	95%

Calculating Amount Needed

Assume you need the following quantities, EP, of the indicated fresh fruits. Calculate the AP weight you will need to get the required yield. Numbers 1 to 10 use U.S. amounts; numbers 11 to 20 use metric measures. Complete the calculations assigned by your instructor.

		EP Weight Desired	**AP Weight Needed**
1.	Grapefruit, sectioned	3 lb	_____
2.	Plums	1 lb 12 oz	_____
3.	Kiwi fruit	12 oz	_____
4.	Pineapple	1 lb 12 oz	_____
5.	Peaches	5 lb	_____
6.	Apples	2 lb 4 oz	_____
7.	Cherries, pitted	14 oz	_____
8.	Mangoes	2 lb	_____
9.	Grapes	2 lb 8 oz	_____
10.	Papaya	6 lb 8 oz	_____

	EP Weight Desired	AP Weight Needed
11. Grapefruit, sectioned	1500 g	_____
12. Plums	875 g	_____
13. Kiwi fruit	375 g	_____
14. Pineapple	875 g	_____
15. Peaches	2500 g	_____
16. Apples	1125 g	_____
17. Cherries, pitted	400 g	_____
18. Mangoes	500 g	_____
19. Grapes	1250 g	_____
20. Papaya	3250 g	_____

Calculating Yield

Assume you have the following quantities of the indicated fresh fruits. Calculate the EP weight you will have after trimming. Numbers 21 to 30 use U.S. amounts; numbers 31 to 40 use metric measures. Complete the calculations assigned by your instructor.

	AP Weight	EP Weight
21. Coconut	2 lb	_____
22. Apricots	14 oz	_____
23. Watermelon	7 lb	_____
24. Apples	3 lb 8 oz	_____
25. Kiwi fruit	2 lb 12 oz	_____
26. Grapefruit, sectioned	5 lb 8 oz	_____
27. Mangoes	3 lb	_____
28. Papaya	5 lb	_____
29. Grapes	2 lb	_____
30. Peaches	1 lb 8 oz	_____

	AP Weight	EP Weight
31. Coconut	1000 g	_____
32. Apricots	400 g	_____
33. Watermelon	3500 g	_____
34. Apples	1750 g	_____
35. Kiwi fruit	1750 g	_____
36. Grapefruit, sectioned	2750 g	_____
37. Mangoes	1500 g	_____
38. Papaya	2500 g	_____
39. Grapes	1000 g	_____
40. Peaches	750 g	_____

D. CALCULATING FORMULA COSTS

Cost out the following formula. For the prices of ingredients, use figures supplied by your instructor or taken from the Appendix, "Sample Prices," in this Study Guide. The problem is given in both U.S. and metric measures. Complete the problem assigned by your instructor.

Item: Apple Crisp

Yield: 48 portions, 4 oz each

Ingredients	Amount	Amount in Converted Units	EP Unit Cost ($)	Total ($)
Apples, AP	10 lb 8 oz	_____	_____	_____
Sugar	4 oz	_____	_____	_____
Lemon juice	2 fl oz	_____	_____	_____
Butter	1 lb	_____	_____	_____
Brown sugar	1 lb 8 oz	_____	_____	_____
Cinnamon	0.12 oz	_____	_____	_____
Pastry flour	1 lb 8 oz	_____	_____	_____
		Total cost		_____
		Quantity produced		_____
		Cost per portion		_____

Item: Apple Crisp

Yield: 48 portions, 120 g each

Ingredients	Amount	Amount in Converted Units	EP Unit Cost ($)	Total ($)
Apples, AP	5400 g	_____	_____	_____
Sugar	125 g	_____	_____	_____
Lemon juice	60 mL	_____	_____	_____
Butter	500 g	_____	_____	_____
Brown sugar	750 g	_____	_____	_____
Cinnamon	4 g	_____	_____	_____
Pastry flour	750 g	_____	_____	_____
		Total cost		_____
		Quantity produced		_____
		Cost per portion		_____

Chapter 23
Dessert Presentation

This chapter is different from all the others in the book in that it contains no mixing methods or baking procedures. Rather, it is devoted primarily to suggestions for various dessert platings. Beginning with a number of general guidelines, you will learn how to best approach the design of attractive dessert presentations. After studying the guidelines and the individual examples, you are encouraged to let your imagination go to work to develop your own ideas for offering desserts that are as good to look at as they are to eat.

After studying Chapter 23, you should be able to:

1. Understand the importance of good basic baking and pastry skills and professional work habits to the art of plating desserts.

2. Understand why it is important to consider the convenience and expectations of the customer when planning dessert presentations.

3. Match main dessert items, secondary items, and sauces to create an appealing balance of flavor, texture, temperature, color, and shape in plated desserts.

4. List secondary items and garnishes commonly used to enhance plated desserts.

5. Apply sauces to dessert plates in attractive and appropriate ways.

6. Plate desserts attractively and appropriately for a variety of food service venues.

DESSERT PRESENTATIONS

Review the principles outlined in the text, then draw diagrams for four dessert presentations, using the examples in the text for guidance. In the blanks provided, for each presentation list the main items, secondary items, and sauces you plan to use. Make your selections from recipes in the text, from class handouts, or from resources assigned by your instructor.

For the first two presentations, draw your diagrams in the large circles provided, which represent round plates. For the second two presentations no plate outlines are provided. Draw plates of any shape desired or assigned (round, oval, square, and so on).

Presentation 1

Main item(s) _____   Secondary items and décor

_____   _____

_____   _____

Sauce(s) _____   _____

_____   _____

Presentation 2

Main item(s) _____

_____

_____

Secondary items and décor

_____

_____

_____

Sauce(s) _____

_____

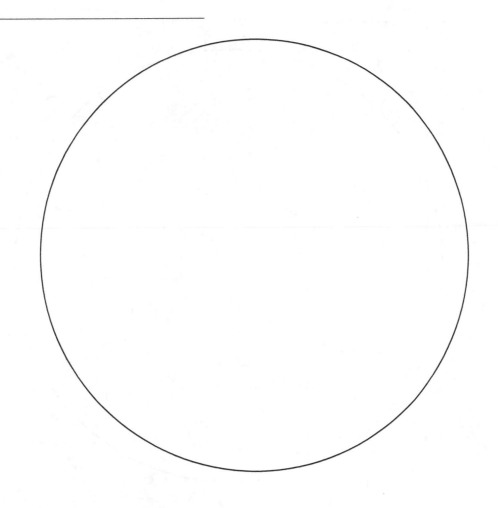

Presentation 3

Main item(s) _____

_____

_____

Secondary items and décor

_____

_____

_____

Sauce(s) _____

_____

Presentation 4

Main item(s) _____

_____

_____

Secondary items and décor

_____

_____

_____

Sauce(s) _____

_____

Chapter 24

Chocolate

Chapters 24, 25, and 26 introduce you to a number of advanced decorative techniques, many of which are very difficult and require demonstration and guidance from your instructor, followed by a great deal of practice. The first of these three chapters explains how to work with chocolate for the purpose of making decorative items and confections.

After studying Chapter 24, you should be able to:

1. Temper chocolate couverture.

2. Use tempered chocolate for dipping and molding.

3. Produce a variety of chocolate decorations.

4. Make chocolate truffles.

A.   TERMS

Fill in each blank with the term that is defined or described.

_____	1.	A whitish coating on chocolate, caused by separated cocoa butter.
_____	2.	Natural, sweet chocolate containing no added fats other than natural cocoa butter; used for dipping, molding, coating, and similar purposes.
_____	3.	A thick paste made of chocolate and glucose, which can be molded by hand into various shapes.
_____	4.	The process of melting and cooling chocolate to prepare it for molding or dipping.
_____	5.	In the manufacturing of chocolate, the process of grinding together cocoa, cocoa butter, and sugar to create a fine, smooth texture.
_____	6.	A method for carrying out the process described in number 4 by spreading the melted chocolate back and forth on a marble slab.
_____	7.	The fat component of natural chocolate.
_____	8.	Unsweetened chocolate consisting of cocoa solids plus the substance described in number 7.

B.   SHORT-ANSWER QUESTIONS

1.   Melted chocolate that is to be used for dipping can be thinned out by adding _____.

2.   The two basic components of unsweetened chocolate are _____ and _____.

3.   The three basic components of sweet chocolate are _____, _____, and _____.

4.   The four basic components of milk chocolate are _____, _____, _____, and _____.

5.   To temper chocolate, first melt it and bring it to a temperature of _____ _____.

6.   After the chocolate is melted, the next stage of tempering is to _____ _____.

7.   Finally, to prepare the tempered chocolate for dipping or molding, it should be _____ _____ _____.

8.   If a whitish coating appears on the cooled chocolate, it probably means that, during the step described in number 7, the chocolate was _____ _____.

9.   If chocolate that has been tempered takes too long to harden, it probably means that _____ _____ _____.

10.   When dipping chocolates, a good temperature for the work area is _____ _____.

11.   Briefly describe how to dip candies using a dipping fork in order to coat them with chocolate.
       _____
       _____
       _____

12.   Piping chocolate is made of tempered chocolate mixed with _____ until it forms the proper consistency.

13. Describe how to make modeling chocolate. _____

_____

_____

14. How should chocolate molds be prepared to ensure that they are clean and free of scratches? _____

_____

_____

15. Why can chocolate usually be removed from molds easily (providing the chocolate was properly tempered and the molds are in good condition and were prepared properly)?

_____

_____

16. If you spilled a few drops of water into chocolate while it is being melted, it would

_____.

17. Very simple chocolate truffles can be made out of only two ingredients,

_____ and _____.

Chapter 25

Marzipan, Nougatine, and Pastillage

Your study of decorative work continues in this chapter, which covers marzipan, nougatine, and pastillage. The first two are not only used for purely decorative work; they can also be used to make edible confections, garnishes, and components for many kinds of desserts. Pastillage, on the other hand, even though it is made out of edible ingredients, is used only for decorations and display pieces. It is not intended to be eaten.

After studying Chapter 25, you should be able to:

1. Make and handle marzipan, and mold decorative items from it.

2. Make pastillage and use it to create decorative items.

3. Make nougatine and shape it into simple decorative items.

A. TERMS

Fill in each blank with the term that is defined or described.

_____ 1. A sugar paste made of sugar, starch, and gelatin, which is used for decorative work, and which becomes hard and brittle when dry.

_____ 2. A mixture of caramelized sugar and almonds or other nuts; used in decorative work and as a confection and flavoring.

_____ 3. The material described in number 1, but made with vegetable gums instead of gelatin.

_____ 4. A paste or confection made of ground almonds and sugar, often used for decorative work.

B. MARZIPAN REVIEW

1. In the space below, list the ingredients for making marzipan. Then describe the procedure for making marzipan, using numbered steps.

2. When working with pastry doughs, you use flour to dust the work surface. When working with marzipan, you use _____ to dust the work surface.

3. Mixing bowls for marzipan should be made of _____.

   The reason for this is _____

   _____

   _____

   _____

   _____.

4. How should marzipan be stored? _____

   _____

   _____

   _____

   _____

C. REVIEW OF PASTILLAGE AND NOUGATINE

1. In the space below, list the ingredients for making pastillage. Then describe the procedure for making pastillage, using numbered steps.

2. Mixing bowls for making pastillage should be made of _____.
   The reason for this is that_____
   _____.

3. When working with pastillage, the work surface should be dusted with _____
   _____.

4. When working with pastillage, unused portions should be stored by _____
   _____
   _____.

5. Describe a simple method for making a pastillage bowl. _____
   _____
   _____
   _____

6.	How should molded pastillage pieces be dried? _____

	_____

7.	If a pastillage showpiece is made of more than one piece, the parts are fastened together by

	_____.

8.	Nougatine pieces are fastened together by _____

	_____.

9.	The two main ingredients in nougatine are _____
	and _____.

10.	The best work surface for rolling and cutting nougatine is a(n) _____.

	The next best choice is a(n) _____ that
	has been _____ so that the nougatine won't stick.

11.	The basic tool for cutting nougatine is _____.

12.	Nougatine can be molded like pastillage, but if it becomes too hard to mold it can be
	softened by _____.

Chapter 26
Sugar Techniques

Pastry chefs often consider decorative sugar work to be one of the pinnacles of their art. In this chapter, you are introduced to the fine art of making beautiful display pieces with pulled and blown sugar. In addition, you learn to use boiled sugar to make a number of simple, practical items that aren't as challenging as pulled sugar and that can be used every day to create interesting decorations and garnishes. Finally, you are introduced to some basic candies made with the sugar boiling techniques you have learned.

After studying Chapter 26, you should be able to:

1. Boil sugar syrups correctly for decorative sugar works.

2. Make spun sugar, sugar cages, and poured sugar.

3. Pull sugar and use it to make simple pulled- and blown-sugar decorative items.

4. Prepare basic boiled sugar confections.

A. TERMS

Fill in each blank with the term that is defined or described.

_____ 1. Sugar that is boiled to the hard-crack stage, allowed to harden slightly, then pulled or stretched until it develops a pearly sheen.

_____ 2. The material described in number 1, which is then made into hollow shapes by being blown up like a balloon.

_____ 3. Boiled sugar made into fine, hairlike threads.

_____ 4. Sugar that is boiled to the hard-crack stage and then poured into molds to harden.

_____ 5. A chemical process in which a double sugar splits into two simple sugars.

_____ 6. A confection made in a similar fashion as fondant, most often flavored with chocolate.

_____ 7. A sugar substitute, derived from sugar, that can be melted and worked like cast sugar and pulled sugar.

B. SHORT-ANSWER QUESTIONS

1. Using numbered steps, describe the procedure for boiling sugar to make pulled sugar.

2. Two major factors that affect the hardness of a finished pulled sugar piece are:

    (a) _____

    (b) _____

3. Two precautions that should be observed to keep a boiling syrup from discoloring are:

    (a) _____

    (b) _____

4. A simple mold that can be used to make sugar cages is a(n) _____.

5. To keep a sugar cage from sticking to the mold on which it is made, you should

    _____.

6. In the space below, briefly describe how to make spun sugar.

7. Pulled sugar gets its name from the way it is manipulated. Describe how this is done.

    _____

    _____

    _____

    This manipulation is done just until _____

    _____.

8. If sugar is pulled too much, it will _____

    _____.

9. While it is waiting to be shaped, pulled sugar is kept soft by _____

    _____.

10. For the clearest, most colorless product, what kind of water should be mixed with isomalt
    when cooking it? _____

11. Isomalt should be cooked to a temperature of _____ to prepare it for
    decorative work.

12. After isomalt is cooked to the proper temperature and the cooking is stopped, it should be

    _____

    _____

    so that it is free of bubbles.

Chapter 27

Baking for Special Diets

Dietary concerns are becoming more important in the lives of many people, so chefs and bakers are paying more attention to these concerns. Food service workers are learning to help their customers eat more healthfully while still enjoying desserts, breads, and other treats. Even more important, cooks and bakers are learning to help customers with allergies avoid foods that can be extremely dangerous for them. This chapter introduces you to the most important concepts of baking for special diets.

After studying Chapter 27, you should be able to:

1. Identify and describe nutritional concerns associated with baked goods and desserts.

2. Identify and describe allergy and food intolerance concerns associated with baked goods and desserts.

3. Identify the three ways to modify an ingredient in a baking formula to make the formula suitable for a specialized diet.

4. Using a knowledge of ingredient functions, describe how to reduce or eliminate fat, sugar, gluten, and dairy products in baking formulas.

A.   TERMS

Fill in each blank with the term that is defined or described.

_____   1.   A vegetarian diet that excludes all animal products, including dairy products and eggs.

_____   2.   A vegetarian diet that allows dairy products and eggs.

_____   3.   A vegetarian diet that allows milk and other dairy products.

_____   4.   A solid fat, usually manufactured by hydrogenation, that limits the body's ability to rid itself of cholesterol.

_____   5.   A substance that triggers an allergic reaction.

_____   6.   A sudden and severe allergic reaction of the immune system.

_____   7.   Any of a group of nutrients essential for growth, for building body tissue, and for basic body functions; can also be used for energy if the diet doesn't contain enough carbohydrates and fats.

_____   8.   The amount of heat needed to raise the temperature of 1 kilogram of water 1 degree Celsius; used as a measure of food energy.

_____   9.   A type of complex carbohydrate that is not absorbed by the body but is necessary for the proper functioning of the digestive system.

_____   10. A fatty substance found in foods derived from animal products and in the human body; too high a level of this substance has been linked to heart disease.

_____   11. A food that provides few nutrients per calorie.

_____   12. An allergic reaction to gluten in which the lining of the intestine is damaged.

_____   13. The quantity of nutrients per calorie.

_____   14. A nonallergic reaction to a food that may be characterized by any of a variety of undesirable symptoms.

_____   15. A food component that is essential for the functioning or growth of an organism.

_____   16. Any of a group of compounds, including starches and sugars, that supply energy to the body.

_____   17. A fat that is normally solid at room temperature.

_____   18. Any of a group of compounds present in foods in very small quantities and necessary for regulating body functions.

_____   19. Any of a group of compounds consisting of chains of fatty acids that supply energy to the body in a concentrated form.

_____   20. A type of synthetic sweetener derived from sucrose.

B.   SHORT-ANSWER QUESTIONS

1.   Give two examples of foods with high nutrient density.

_____

_____

Give two examples of foods with low nutrient density.

_____

_____

2. List the six categories of nutrients.

(a)_____

(b)_____

(c)_____

(d)_____

(e)_____

(f)_____

3. List six examples of ways ingredients of breads and pastries can be modified to increase their nutritional content.

(a)_____

(b)_____

(c)_____

(d)_____

(e)_____

(f)_____

4. Name two categories of vegetarian diets that allow eggs.

(a)_____

(b)_____

5. In the space below, explain how cross-contamination in a bakeshop can pose a hazard for customers suffering from a food allergy.

6. Of all food allergies, which one poses the greatest challenge for bakers? Why?

_____

_____

_____

7. Identify the three ways to modify an ingredient in a baking formula to make it suitable for a specialized diet.

(a) _____

_____

(b) _____

_____

(c) _____

_____

8. What are the four primary functions of basic bakeshop ingredients? After each function, list the ingredients included in that category.

(a) _____

(b) _____

(c) _____

(d) _____

9. When you reduce the amount of fat in a formula to make it suitable for a special diet, what two basic techniques can you use to make sure that the formula you have changed is still in balance? Give examples of each.

(a) _____

_____

_____

(b) _____

_____

_____

10. What milk substitutes are available for people with milk allergies?

_____

_____

_____

11. For each of the following ingredients, circle Yes if that ingredient is suitable for use in a gluten-free diet. Circle No if it is not.

Yes	No	Cornstarch
Yes	No	Arrowroot
Yes	No	Potato starch
Yes	No	Rye flour
Yes	No	Barley flour
Yes	No	Rice flour
Yes	No	Oat flour
Yes	No	Soy flour
Yes	No	Tapioca flour
Yes	No	Buckwheat flour
Yes	No	Chick pea (garbanzo) flour
Yes	No	Malt
Yes	No	Spelt flour
Yes	No	Semolina

Appendix
Sample Prices

Your instructor(s) may want you to use the prices on current invoices when you do the Formula Cost exercises in this manual. If not, you may use the following hypothetical prices. Do not worry about whether or not these prices seem realistic. Prices change, but you can still practice the calculations using these numbers.

Almond paste	$12.00 per lb	$26.50 per kg
Almonds, powdered	13.00 per lb	28 60 per kg
Apples, AP	1.50 per lb	3.30 per kg
Baking powder	4.00 per lb	8.80 per kg
Butter	2.00 per lb	4.20 per kg
Chocolate, dark sweet	5.50 per lb	12.00 per kg
Chocolate, unsweetened	5.95 per lb	13.00 per kg
Cinnamon	1.50 per oz	5.30 per 100 g
Cornstarch	0.69 per lb	1.50 per kg
Cream, heavy	2.95 per qt	2.95 per L
Eggs, whole, bulk	1.00 per lb	2.20 per kg
Eggs, whites, bulk	0.90 per lb	2.00 per kg
Eggs, yolks, bulk	1.20 per lb	2.65 per kg
Flour, bread	0.25 per lb	0.55 per kg
Flour, cake	0.35 per lb	0.75 per kg
Flour, pastry	0.30 per lb	0.65 per kg
Honey	2.20 per lb	4.65 per kg
Lemon juice	2.00 per pt	4.00 per L
Milk, whole	0.75 per qt	0.75 per L
Nonfat milk solids,	4.50 per lb	10.00 per kg
Nutmeg	1.45 per oz	5.00 per 100 g
Oil (vegetable)	5.20 per gal	1.30 per L
Raisins	1.25 per lb	2.75 per kg
Rum	15.00 per qt	15.00 per L

Salt	$0.25 per lb	$0.55 per kg
Shortening, regular	0.65 per lb	1.45 per kg
Sugar, brown	0.60 per lb	1.35 per kg
Sugar, confectioners'	0.65 per lb	1.45 per kg
Sugar, granulated	0.40 per lb	1.00 per kg
Vanilla extract	20.00 per qt	20.00 per L
Yeast, fresh	4.00 per lb	8.80 per kg